LAURA ASHLEY
LIVING ROOMS

LAURA ASHLEY
LIVING ROOMS

KATE CORBETT-WINDER

HARMONY BOOKS

New York

Published by Harmony Books, a division of Crown Publishers, Inc.,
225 Park Avenue South, New York, New York 10003.

Published in Great Britain by George Weidenfeld & Nicolson
Limited, 91 Clapham High Street, London SW4 7TA, England.

HARMONY and Colophon are trademarks of Crown Publishers, Inc.

LAURA ASHLEY and logo are trademarks of Laura Ashley
Manufacturing BV

Manufactured in Italy

Library of Congress Cataloguing-in-Publication Data

Corbett-Winder. Kate

    Laura Ashley Living Rooms
        p.   cm.
    Bibliography: p.
    Includes index.
    1. Living rooms.   2. Interior decoration.   3. Laura Ashley
(Firm)
I. Corbett-Winder. Kate.   II. Title
NK2117.L5B86   1989
747.7.5.0942—dc19   87-18135
ISBN 0-517-56857-8
10 9 8 7 6 5 4 3 2 1
First American Edition

CONTENTS

*Cottage garden sweet peas, either climbing walls
or scenting the mantelpiece, bring the country spirit inside.*

INTRODUCTION

This book is intended as a source of inspiration and ideas for creating a living room that complements your surroundings and way of life. Whether you live in a rambling country house or cottage, a city terrace or flat, it is your living room that creates a first impression. Like a barometer of your character and lifestyle, it reflects an atmosphere that can be traditional or modern, romantic or practical, grand and formal or cosy and casual.

The style you choose to establish should be compatible with the intended role of the living room. Your way of life and its priorities are the essential guidelines, determining the mood and nature of the living room. Should it become an elegant drawing room to suit the needs of formal entertaining, or a more cosy sitting room to use for informal occasions and everyday family relaxation? Does your lifestyle dictate the need for a room with a quiet contemplative air conducive to reading or listening to music, or a general family room for watching television, playing games and eating informal meals?

Each chapter looks at a particular role of the living room, and explores the range of decorative possibilities for the walls, windows, furnishings, floors and essential accessories within each room, combining current ideas and past traditions to create a comfortable interior, compatible with the varied demands of contemporary life.

To create a formal drawing room, borrow inspiration from the classical proportions of an eighteenth-century French *salon*; for a more intimate sitting room, try a Victorian atmosphere — plied with pattern, rich colour, romantic drapery and ornament — or the abstract profusion of Bloomsbury style. A small room that catches the early sunlight prompts images of a Regency morning room, while a study or sitting room with a traditional bookish air can be modelled on a comfortable country-house library. Today's multifunctional spaces, be they open-plan studio apartments or family living rooms, draw on practical solutions to modern-day needs with flair and ingenuity, while a garden room or conservatory indulges a perennial passion for gardening and evokes a feeling of Mediterranean warmth.

Colour, texture and pattern are evocative elements of decoration, establishing an air of comfortable permanence as well as setting the mood, whether this is formal or casual, contemporary or evocative of past eras.

This book illustrates the Laura Ashley tradition of looking to the past for inspiration, whether recreated in authentic detail, accurate to the last trimming, or used as a catalyst to stimulate the imagination. Classic florals, fruit prints, stripes, sprigs and geometrics derived from period wallpapers, tapestries, scraps of dress materials and furnishing fabrics combine with sources from across the globe: from oriental and Moorish cultures to European and American folk art.

However imaginative the decoration, a room needs time to evolve. Like painting a picture, the finishing touches cannot all be decided in advance. A room that has established itself by degrees feels well-loved and lived in, never too contrived and perfect. The decorative ideas that follow are diverse, but they all encapsulate the essence of comfort and the belief that a living room should be a welcoming source of pleasure and relaxation.

THE DRAWING ROOM

The drawing room has always been the smartest, most lavishly decorated part of the house. Today it is still the room that gives an instant insight into your tastes, possessions and lifestyle, while conveying a formal atmosphere that is appropriate for entertaining.

The drawing room evolved from the grand *salons* of sixteenth-century Europe: a time when the home was a stage set for lavish entertaining rather than somewhere comfortable in which to live, a showcase for the tastes of the day, and a place to display the latest style of interior decoration and furnishings. The equivalent in grand English homes was the saloon or great chamber, also used for large receptions, dining and dancing. But it was the English quest for privacy and relaxation towards the end of the eighteenth century that created the drawing room as we know it today. Reception rooms were now built on ground level rather than on the first floor, and furniture was moved from the walls into the centre of the room, revolutionizing the atmosphere and role of the drawing room. Throughout history drawing-rooms have been a barometer of style with interiors reflecting the moral, social, and political mood of the time. Freed from any obligation to be in fashion today, we can draw upon every aspect of period décor to create an elegant room in keeping with both our homes and lifestyles.

The Georgian drawing room, for example, was influenced by the Grand Tour; the Classic rule of taste, as portrayed by Palladio, guided drawing-room decoration and influenced such figures as Sheraton, Chippendale and Adam. Decorative styles including rococo, chinoiserie and medieval Gothic lent an air of the whimsical, the exotic and the romantic.

The elegance of Jane Austen's drawing rooms sums up the style of the Regency, with its gentle arts of sketching and music-making that contributed to a contrived informality.

The lived-in look was the essence of the Victorian drawing room, with its abundance of sofas, ottomans and couches. The period is full of ideas for today from curtain designs and wall decoration to trimmings.

The past is a constant source of inspiration for interior decorators. But what makes professionals like John Fowler, Nancy Lancaster and Geoffrey Bennison legendary, is an unconventional approach to tradition as well as the essential confidence, sense of humour and talent with which they mixed elements to create an original, inviting drawing room.

RIGHT An eighteenth-century drawing room that captures the Georgian spirit of dignity and elegance. Upright furniture ranged against the wall gives prominence to the architectural features of fireplace, dado, cornice, shuttered sash windows and symmetrical decorative detail.

BELOW The bold floral panels in this Georgian-style drawing room add a contemporary dimension to the original mouldings, while characteristic jade paintwork, exposed floorboards and simple damask curtains remain true to the period.

In this chapter, we look at the various ways of decorating the drawing room to suit individual needs and situations, ranging from the formal elegance of a Georgian-style interior to the more comfortable, yet still smart, drawing rooms of modern city life.

Choosing a Style to Suit the Room

In choosing a decorative style that is appropriate to the scale, setting and function of your drawing room, the shape and architectural structure of the room are useful guidelines. Tall, well-proportioned rooms with classical architraves, large sash windows and a dominant fireplace inspire symmetrical Georgian-style treatment. More irregular shapes with alcoves, bay windows and recesses, complete with ceiling rose, suggest Victorian styles. Pointed arched windows, doors and fitments conjure Gothic eccentricity.

Having chosen a style, it is important not to feel constricted by it. Use a period style, for example, as a source of inspiration, not as a fixed rule. In every period there are key details that convey a particular atmosphere; consider the print designs, fabrics and colour schemes that characterize the mood; the furniture arrangement, the lighting, the floor treatment, the shape of curtain and pelmet, the style of picture hanging, and then add your imagination to the scheme.

Formal Elegance

Symmetry and balanced proportions provide a natural framework for today's formal drawing room. A classical sense of order and harmony creates an elegant, dignified atmosphere, to play up or down depending on the scale of your drawing room. Architectural features such as carved mouldings, plasterwork ceilings, pedimented doors, fireplaces, architraves, columns and pilasters are the backbone of a formal scheme, recreating the splendours of

William Kent or Robert Adam.

Drawing rooms with these existing features have a tangible eighteenth-century quality, but inbuilt architectural details are not essential. Decoration can convey as well as enhance a sense of structured space and elegance. The use of paper borders and painted panels can improvise a framework, while symmetrically arranged furniture, ornaments and paired picture-hanging all help instate classical order.

Creating the Style

Colour Schemes Colour is a simple yet potent way to recall period atmosphere. A Georgian palette, for example, falls into two groups: the ceremonial crimson, dark green and deep smoke blue of the mid century, embellished with gold leaf and marble, or the spectrum of muted but intense pastels that followed – the lavender grey, butter yellow and pale jade, reminiscent of Adam interiors.

Today it is the soft faded versions of those original, surprisingly bright colours that conjure the mood. A large formal drawing room can carry off an expanse of crimson, but in smaller spaces a lighter scheme based on cowslip yellow, duck-egg blue or jade green gives a fresh elegance. Georgian style has a serenity, evoked by a scheme of one dominant colour combined with closely related tones, like a picture painted in tones of one colour. Alternatively, two hues of similar tone can be paired harmoniously; perhaps aquamarine with apricot, pale cowslip with buttermilk, or neutral hues of cream and sand.

Walls and Windows

Architectural Features Walls are a distinctive feature of the room, defined by a cornice and dado rail (originally fixed to prevent furniture marking the walls). As these hall-marks give a room immediate grandeur and supply the framework for a formal decorative scheme, it is well worth creating the effect on smooth modern walls. With ingenuity, wooden beading can be used as a simple dado rail, suggesting the original demarcation between wall hangings and panelled dado, or below the ceiling as a cornice or picture rail.

A wallpaper that gives the illusion of texture – a close stippled or dappled print – recreates the tonal weave of watered silk or fine woollen hangings that dominated drawing-room walls in the eighteenth century. An authentic touch is to hang wallpaper in panels, edging each frame with a fillet – originally a carved border of gilded wood or papier mâché. A contemporary version of gimp or braid adds a sense of symmetry and definition to the walls, a feeling that could be accentuated by continuing the fillet along a dado rail.

For an extra touch of extravagance, run a deep decorative fringe along the cornice to form a border, in true eighteenth-century style, perhaps echoing the colours of trimmings on curtains or upholstery.

Paint Finishes Paintwork is an alternative to wallpaper. The decorative finishes that are popular today are rooted in Georgian drawing rooms, where mouldings were elaborately picked out in toning colours, or white and gold leaf for a more ornate effect. *Trompe-l'oeil* paintwork can be brought into play with walls, doors or dado painted in tones of one colour to look like panels. Avoid the flat look of uniform paint cover by sponging or dragging one shade over another to give a sense of texture and depth to the walls. Marbling gives a classical allusion to skirtings in a strain that blends with the colour scheme – perhaps a warm yellow sienna streaked with brown, cool white Carrara with grey veins or brilliant green malachite or darker Verde Antico.

A cornice can be created with paint, paper or fabric. A classical Greek key border will give a formal look.

A fabric cornice enriched with fringing and tassels recreates a grand period effect.

The lines of a delicate Regency moulding can be picked out in pastel paintwork.

A paper border in a pretty scroll design of leaves and flowers creates a deep, Victorian-style cornice.

ABOVE *This elaborate window dressing, with its contrasting swagged and tasselled silk curtains and ruched voile blind, retains a light romantic touch, typical of the fashion set by early nineteenth-century France.*

RIGHT *A tall window hung with rich gilded damask introduces an element of Georgian splendour to the drawing room. The distressed gold rod, carved finial and silk fringed pelmet, set against a* trompe l'oeil *marble wall, heighten the sumptuous effect.*

Curtains and Blinds Treatments should have an elegant simplicity that enhances the characteristic sash windows and unifies the walls with related pattern and texture. Window decoration was in its infancy in the early eighteenth century, relying on shutters for insulation and a flat 'sash' blind of linen or taffeta to filter strong sunlight. The earliest decorative style was a reefed pull-up curtain hung below a boxed pelmet – the forerunner of today's festoon blind.

Full-length curtains are more dignified in a formal drawing room, although the two elements could be combined at a large window, using an important damask print for the curtains and pelmet, with a small-scale companion print, plain cotton or voile for the

festoon blind. The most classic pelmets are looped into swags, with tapered tails hanging down each side of the curtain.

Furniture and Furnishings

Positioning Furniture Furniture, its style and its arrangement, contributes to the mood. Furnishing a drawing room with genuine antiques is an expensive impossibility for most people, but you can evoke the right atmosphere by giving the room a definite sense of order. Arranging furniture and ornaments in pairs conveys a formality that does not detract from comfort. Consider a pair of classic sofas at right angles to the fireplace, for example, with matching occasional tables at either end and a pair of large table lamps with elegant pleated shades.

Furnishings Drawing-room furnishings can convey a co-ordinated feel, reflecting without exactly matching the colour and texture of the walls and curtains. The period ideal of uniform pattern may seem too neat and contrived today. Instead of identical upholstery or loose covers, establish an unmistakable continuity between sofas and armchairs, keeping a close range of colour and print in diverse fabrics that range from fine chintz to substantial ribbed ottoman.

Fringing, an eighteenth-century decorative device to smarten everyday protective covers, adds a degree of elegance to both loose covers and upholstered chairs. Co-ordinating gimp or braid can be used to the same effect. The eighteenth-century scheme of changing summer and winter wall hangings can be adapted to drawing-room loose covers. A pale ivory satin-weave damask or buttermilk chintz could be exchanged for a burgundy linen union or ottoman, giving a warm rich atmosphere in winter.

TOP *Chinoiserie porcelain adds decorative detail to a drawing-room mantelpiece, given definition by a china-blue fillet of rope-headed gimp that links the painted fire surround and finely mottled wallpaper.*

ABOVE *Attention to detail establishes a sense of unity in a room. The braid trim on this mahogany chair back relates the upholstery to the smoke-blue stippled walls.*

Floor and Fireplace

Floor A drawing-room floor is an important consideration. Waxed floor boards, or a pale ground carpet overlaid with a tapestried or faded antique rug, lend an air of underplayed grandeur that recalls the dry scrubbed wooden boards of an eighteenth-century *salon* with its tapestry-weave Aubusson or Savonnerie carpet.

Fireplace This gives an essential focus to the room — perhaps a traditional Adam-style example of marble, or painted or waxed wood with carved mouldings, festoons and roundels in the classical spirit. A marbled paint finish gives a standard fireplace an elegant facelift. A mantelshelf can continue the idea of symmetry, displaying pairs of ornaments, candlesticks and cornucopias brimming with flowers. An empty hearth could be screened by a painted chimney board or decorated with a basket of dried flowers.

Lighting

The style of lighting enhances atmosphere. Candlelight, the sole source of illumination before 1800, summons a romantic mood for special occasions with tall white or gold candles burning in elegant candelabras or gilded sconces. To be more practical, a central chandelier or wall brackets fitted with candle bulbs can be dimmed to a gentle glow.

Decorative Details

Pictures are a key detail, hung in symmetrical pairs or sets. Hang the tallest picture level with the tallest piece of furniture, so that the tops of the frames form a straight, even line across the wall, a rule employed by Georgian designers. Large gilded mirrors above the fireplace add authentic elegance, casting reflected light into the room. Or hang a mirror on the pier wall between windows to recall the early eighteenth-century 'triad' of the French *salon*, where a console table stood before a pier glass, flanked by ornate candlestands.

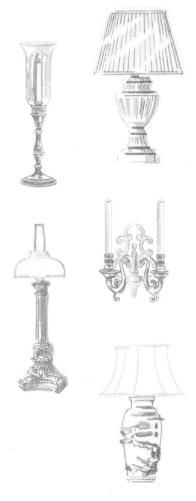

Lighting is an evocative means of creating atmosphere: a classical ribbed urn lamp is enhanced by a generous pleated shade; a candle burning in an elliptical glass shade casts a gentle reflective glow; delicate sconces, hung in pairs, heighten a mood of formal elegance; an early Victorian oil lamp adds decorative authenticity to a period scheme; Chinese vases make elegant lamp bases, topped with a pale curved shade.

A Softer, Romantic Look

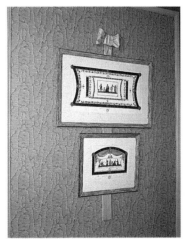

An air of sophistication can still prevail in the drawing room, but with softer lines and a more relaxed atmosphere, redolent of the Regency. A delightful aspect of this style of drawing room is a strong bond with nature. The Picturesque concept of architecture at the end of the eighteenth century kindled a romantic view of the countryside, affecting interior arrangements as much as exterior. The view from a room became a significant feature.

Creating the Style

A spirit of freshness is evoked by French windows that lead from a drawing room straight into the garden or conservatory, embracing nature as an integral part of decoration. Fresh flowers are essential to the style, with an extravagance recalling the elaborate floral swags festooned around candelabras or the rows of potted box trees flanking the walk from interior to garden. Bold floral prints strewn across curtains, upholstery and cushions accentuate the garden spirit – an effect which can be intensified by matching a profusion of fresh flowers to the fabric at the appropriate season.

Colour Classic schemes revolve around one dominant colour. Vivid shades of butter yellow, apple green, coral, rose or sapphire blue blended with white (fashionable during the Regency classical revival as a sign of purity and virtue) or diluted tones of the key colour give the drawing room a fresh, feminine atmosphere.

Walls and Windows

Wallpapers and Borders Wallpapers that simulate the chintzes and draped silks used in

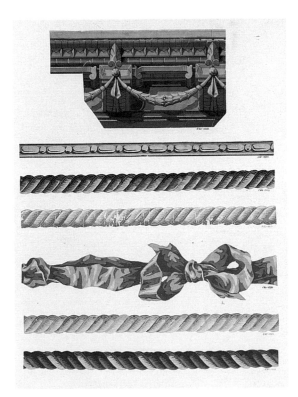

Regency interiors sum up the mood. Use a two-tone wallpaper that suggests the ripple of watered silks; or subtle stripes of duck-egg blue, coral or yellow, or a pattern combining stripes on a spotted background. A classical border can accentuate a cornice or skirting (the dado was not a feature of the Regency interior). In a tall room, the ceiling too could be painted, perhaps in a soft shade of the master colour, with any mouldings picked out in white.

Curtains and Pelmets Windows are a focal point of the drawing room with luxurious curtains that reflect the wall treatment. Consider a corresponding floral cotton or chintz against stippled walls, or a plain chintz against striped wallpaper. The curtains need to be extravagant, hanging to the floor in generous folds, with swags and tails, fringed pelmets or continued drapery extending from one window to the next.

Furniture and Furnishings

An almost tangible sense of gracious ease can be evoked with elegant *chaises-longues*, fruit-

A striking combination of coral-striped wallpaper and tasselled floral chintz recalls the Regency affiliation with nature and rich colour. The navy tassel tie-back, looped over the gilded curtain pole, adds a touch of extravagance to the curtains.

FAR LEFT ABOVE *The formality of this drawing room is relaxed by its calm colour scheme and abundance of natural light. It has an uncluttered serenity, instilled by mixing a classical framework with continental furniture and ornament. The traditional wing armchair and ottoman add substantial comfort to the atmosphere.*

FAR LEFT BELOW *The luxurious effect of fabric-covered walls can be conjured with wallpapers that simulate moiré or watered silk.*

Trompe l'oeil *borders of twisted rope, ribbons, braid and classical swags have a three-dimensional quality that can give an almost architectural effect to smooth walls. They also add an original definition of colour and improvised texture to the room, calling attention to windows, shelves and fireplaces, as well as walls and ceilings.*

wood cane-seated chairs, rosewood sofa tables, card tables and delicate work-boxes positioned informally around the room. Applied decoration is prominent on painted and 'faux bamboo' furniture, *petit point* firescreens, lacquer and penwork, reflecting the accomplishments of a Regency lady.

Striped upholstery is a characteristic fea-

This Chippendale-style armchair with Regency Gothick fretwork and striped upholstery contrasts with the feminine flounced chintz cushion. A rope-work border along the skirting gives classical balance to the composition.

RIGHT *A room that recalls the ostentatious splendours of French Empire style, with its robust colours, bold striped walls, ornate swagged curtains and heavily bolstered day bed, inviting long hours of relaxation*

ture of the drawing room, originally enhancing the sabre-like curves of Grecian couches and daybeds. A more contemporary effect can be recreated with striped cotton loose covers on sofas, chairs and upholstered seats, or with striped bolsters and piped squab cushions tied to the backs of cane-seated chairs with bows in a co-ordinating colour.

Floor and Fireplace

Floor A fitted carpet with a central floral design and contrasting border recalls the floor of an exclusive Regency drawing room. Where rugs are preferred, the exposed floorboards could be painted or grained to resemble a delicate satinwood.

Fireplace The fireplace for this style of drawing room is an elegant feature, less architectural than its Georgian counterpart with a flat chimney breast and narrow mantelpiece. The characteristic carvings or classical swag and urn mouldings of the fire surround are typically of white marble or pale wood with gilded ornamentation. A polished cast-iron grate could be guarded by a pair of Egyptian fire dogs or flanked by bay trees standing in small stone tubs.

Lighting

A light, romantic atmosphere typical of the Regency mood can be suggested by a pair of sconces or candle branches attached to or flanking a gilded mirror on the pier wall, their reflection casting an added glow into the room. These could be supplemented by additional low-level lighting − column table lamps for example, with pleated fabric shades, will throw soft pools of light into different corners of the room.

Decorative Details

Pictures add a definite style; elegant portraits, silhouettes and landscapes in gilded frames could be suspended in vertical tiers. Classical ornaments − marble busts, antiquities, Egyptian or Grecian artefacts − give an authentic flourish to the mantelshelf, bookcase or alcove.

Comfortable Clutter

The Victorian age is a rich source of inspiration. An image of the classic drawing room comes to mind; pattern plied with pattern, plush buttoned sofas, ottomans and couches, tapestried cushions and rugs, velvet and cotton sateen, an imposing black marbled fireplace, and draped grand piano decked with potted ferns and photographs in silver frames. There is an unabashed richness that furnishes the room with a memorable lived-in quality.
Victorian decoration accentuated the drawing room as a female domain: the setting for

morning calls and afternoon teas, where new wealth and status were displayed. An 1833 *Encyclopaedia of Taste and Architecture* by J. C. Loudon advises: 'an elegant drawing room should contain rose pink silk-lined walls with apple green curtains and upholstery'. But sombre colours became more popular later in the century, disguising grime produced by the industrial soot outside and Argand oil lamps and coal fires indoors.

Creating the Style

Colour, Pattern and Fabrics The overstatement of colour and pattern characteristic of this style can be restrained, without losing an opulent effect, by using a more peaceful scheme of corresponding prints and tones. Rich colour schemes of deep crimson, smoke blue, dark green and brown can be lightened with delicate pastels and background tones of sand, ivory or stone.

Authentic prints drawn from original nineteenth-century wallpapers, chintzes and needlepoint evoke a strong period spirit, particularly the fruits and florals, beribboned garlands and birds, and the stylized patterns of Owen Jones and William Morris. The stamped velvet, chenille, silks and cretonne of a Victorian drawing room can be replaced with contemporary fabrics. Cotton sateen, a favourite for curtains and upholstery, has a counterpart in satin-weave cotton, with its smooth sheen and fluid feel that adapts to the curved buttoned upholstery and plentiful drapery. Chintz, originally considered more suitable in a bedroom, can be reinstated on an armchair or frilled curtains, adding a gentle informality to the room.

Walls and Windows

Architectural Details Wall decoration is a key feature, distinguished by the Victorian

divisions, from ceiling to floor, of cornice, frieze, filling, dado and skirting. The amount of pattern you introduce depends on the proportions of the wall. A background paper patterned with a geometric diamond, gothic trefoil, floral or wickerwork trellis can be divided by a corresponding border below the cornice and along the dado rail and skirting. Alternatively, a dado could be papered in a companion print, linked to the filling above with a border. Woodgraining is an important illusion applied to doors and skirting boards, simulating the expensive mahogany found in fashionable drawing rooms.

Curtains and Pelmets Use a stronger colour to contrast with the walls. Consider rich fabrics trailing on the Brussels weave carpet, deep swagged pelmets and elaborate tasselled tie-backs. A matching *portière* curtain — originally intended to exclude draughts and maintain an air of privacy — could be hung across a doorway.

The Moorish quality of the geometric trellis that dominates the wall, tiled floor and door curtain recalls the oriental element that was a strong, particularly masculine, inspiration for Victorian interiors. This scheme of navy, sand and crimson complements the sheen of the grained door, skirting and curtain rod.

FAR LEFT ABOVE *Attention to period detail gives this Victorian drawing room a mood of authentic opulence, emphasized by the profusion of buttoned armchairs, tapestry cushions and regal chaise-duchesse, upholstered in a satin weave that matches the imposing fringed curtains. The crimson and sand colour scheme is carried through with closely related patterns. An Owen Jones geometric wallpaper reflects the chair covers while the border echoes the Gothic quatrefoils on the carpet.*

FAR LEFT BELOW *Rich, heavily fringed fabric, looped over a curtain pole, echoes the grand drapery effects of the nineteenth century.*

The proportion of frieze, filling and dado changed emphasis during Victorian times according to fashionable taste and the scale of a room. A preference for the dado and skirting to appear more substantial than the upper half prompted elaborate relief work coverings of embossed leather, encrusted canvas, linoleum and anaglypta papers.

Pattern plied with pattern – a characteristic abundance of flounced cotton, bolstered and tapestry cushions, banked against paisley, velvet and carved oak. The backdrop of an oriental carpet provides the inspiration for a rich Victorian colour palette.

Furniture and Furnishings

Furniture The proliferation of ottomans, slipper chairs and footstools in the drawing room gives an atmosphere of congested comfort, emphasized by the feminine curves of soft buttoned upholstery. A traditional feature is the large round table where Victorian ladies would read improving books, sew or paint, justifying the leisurely aspect of the room.

Furnishings The preoccupation with draughts and propriety inspired the perennial fashion for floor-length tablecloths; a crisp chintz or cotton cloth edged in a bullion or tasselled fringe can introduce a further companion print to the room. A white lace overcloth gives a fresh look amidst a panoply of colour and pattern, and provides the perfect place for ornaments.

Decorative Trimmings The bullion fringing, tassels, braid and gimp that edge upholstery, pelmets, lampshades and cushions add evocative detail to the room. Embroidered bellpulls are another classic touch, hung above the fireplace flanking a gilt mirror.

Floor and Fireplace

Patterned Floors Pattern is an important dimension of the Victorian floor, adding related colour and print to the overall scheme. A looped Brussels weave carpet with a geometric or floral design and corresponding border has an authentic quality, while smaller tapestried hearth rugs, oriental or imitation turkeywork carpets intensify the patterns and heighten the cosy atmosphere. Exposed floorboards could be stained or grained to a rich mahogany.

Fireplace A Victorian fireplace gives a decorative heart to the room. Its characteristic coal fired cast-iron grate with tiled or marbled fire surround (white statuary or black Belgian) gain period authenticity when cluttered by a helmet-shaped coal scuttle, fire tongs and toasting forks resting on a curly brass fender. Or recreate Victorian drapery with a fringed valance along the mantelpiece that echoes the upholstery fabrics.

Lighting

An overhead chandelier fitted with frosted globes or a hanging oil lamp wired for electricity will recreate a period atmosphere, especially when fitted with a dimmer control to recall the characteristic low lighting of a Victorian drawing room. Cut-glass candle lustres of deep blue Bristol glass, placed on the mantelpiece in front of a large curved mirror, add a flickering brightness to the room at night, backed up by the glow from an Argand-style oil lamp. Lamp bases of tôle, chinoiserie or papier mâché can be given Victorian treatment by the addition of a fringed or tasselled edging to the lampshade – an appropriate period touch.

Decorative Details

The eclectic nature of the drawing room is a significant part of the style. No Victorian-inspired scheme should ignore the potted plants and flowers brought in from the conservatory, the collections of porcelain and glass, the fans, figurines, ribbon plates and objects of papier mâché and mother of pearl.

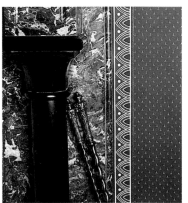

BELOW *As the focus of a drawing room, a Victorian-inspired hearth deserves meticulous attention to detail. Here, the Belgian black marble surround, shiny lacquered column and pokers are enhanced by a Gothic egg and dart border and classic monochrome wallpaper.*

LEFT *This drawing-room corner shows how distinctive Victorian touches can be introduced to a light, uncluttered scheme; notably the fireplace with its cast-iron grate, velvet club fender and tasselled valance along the mantelpiece that echoes the curtain pelmet. The ornate candlesticks, chinoiserie ginger jar, carved overmantle and closely grouped picture arrangement heighten a period effect without letting the room become a set piece.*

Country-house style has a light, gracious quality, achieved by pairing grandeur with more homely elements, floral chintz with checks. An atmosphere of timeless comfort emanates from generous sofas filled with cushions, and a profusion of fresh flowers brings the garden inside.

Country-House Style

A drawing room in the country-house style owes its charm to the past, but it has an eclectic nature that cuts across period definition. While having the appearance of gradual evolution, country-house style is a twentieth-century innovation, born of necessity when country seat finances were at a low ebb between the wars. The drawing room could not sustain its role as a perpetual showcase for smart new furnishings and resorted to the attics to reinstate forgotten antiques and faded heirlooms.

The new tide of decoration was given credence by the legendary John Fowler and his collaborator Nancy Lancaster who perfected the unselfconscious timelessness of this style. Its very charm is the blatant pairing of the grand and the homely to create an immensely comfortable room that can be impressive without being too stately. It is the epitome of grand ease, with a settled atmosphere that comes from a balanced interplay of colour, pattern and content.

Creating the Style

Country-house style has a deceptive nonchalance that reveals a complexity of colour and texture drawn from a contemporary approach to the past. The eighteenth and early nineteenth centuries were a key source of inspiration, but traditions can be turned around, combining unexpected contrasts. A grand treatment might be given to simple cotton ticking, in preference to silk, for example.

Colour and Texture In spite of its disparate nature, there is an instinctive rapport between the furniture in a drawing room and fabric textures: the classic sofas and armchairs, the glorious mix of chintz, tapestry, linen and damask in a diversity of patterns: cabbage roses, stripes, club checks and flamestitch.

Eclectic Elements The ingredients of country-house style have diverse origins and these can throw up surprises too. The traditional Englishness of chintz, linen union, threadbare tapestry carpets, Georgian cabinets, Regency sofa tables and family portraits is often permeated with an element of chinoiserie and the East. John Fowler liked 'a dash of French' in the drawing room to give sophistication and discipline of line amongst informal comfort. A gilded commode or *bergère* chair adds a light elegance, reminiscent of an eighteenth-century château.

Walls and Windows

Paint and Paper The style springs from a traditional setting, but its time-worn effect can be conjured by a clever sense of illusion and improvisation. Wall colour plays an important part. Mellowed tones of butter yellow, sage or apricot can be aged by applying paint in translucent glazes to a white wall. Colour can be blended to a subtle shade, using faded fabrics for inspiration. Alternatively, a bold striped wallpaper in understated tones gives a traditional appearance.

Windows Chintz curtains epitomize country-house style: extravagantly full, with a swagged pelmet trimmed with faded tassels, they create an effect of well-worn grandeur.

Extravagant floral chintz curtains frame a view through French windows to the garden and landscape beyond, emphasizing the natural aspect of country-house style. Butter-yellow walls provide a sunny foil for the Chinese jardinières and complement the soft tones in the needlepoint rug.

A formal arrangement of sofa and armchairs can be lightened with fabric-covered occasional tables, an ideal place for displaying family photographs or vases of cut flowers.

Furniture and Furnishings

Furniture With an absence of heirlooms, improvisation comes into play. Chipboard tables covered in a fringed chintz or cotton cloth make a substitute for antiques, and a surface for lavish flower arrangements. Deep sofas piled with cushions evoke comfort.

Furnishings Loose covers of floral chintz or quiet check linen capture the underplayed country-house look. They were originally devised as protection for the precious upholstery beneath, until considered smart enough by country aristocrats to leave on in everyday company.

The garden is a perennial influence and inspiration for the style. Beside a profusion of fresh flowers and scented plants, flowers from the herbaceous borders can decorate curtains, cushions and loose covers, bringing the delights of the garden inside for years to come.

Floor and Fireplace

Carpets or Floorboards Carpeting the floor in a neutral shade of fawn, a colour christened 'mouse's back' by John Fowler, lays a foundation for the relaxed comfort of the room. It gives a perfect base for tapestried rugs or pastel dhurries that suggest the bleached shades of an Aubusson or Savonnerie carpet. Alternatively, polished parquet or waxed floorboards can be laid with well worn oriental rugs.

Fireplace The country-house-style fireplace has a classic simplicity: a carved wooden fire surround and mantelpiece waxed to a natural sheen or grained or marbled for a grander effect. An open hearth could brim with a basket of fresh flowers, emphasizing the essential country element of this style of drawing room.

Lighting

An antique chandelier catches the spirit of a large country-house drawing room, complemented by a generous number of well placed table lamps with chinoiserie or crackle-glazed ceramic bases and large pale pleated fabric or card shades.

In a smaller setting, wall brackets suggesting gilded sconces are an option, positioned in pairs between windows or flanking the fireplace. A pair of candlesticks adapted into lamps and topped with small parchment shades will cast subtle light from the mantelpiece at night, intensified by a gilded glass overmantel.

Decorative Details

The charm of country-house style is its strongly personal quality. This drawing room reflects its occupants with an informal accumulation of family photographs, eclectic treasures and knick-knacks. Silver and leather framed photographs stand on elegant console tables; collections of porcelain, glass and miniature pictures are displayed on shelves and round tables, amidst vases of fresh garden flowers that scent the room with a country air, even in the town. Family portraits add character to a room, but appear less formal hung without their heavy frames, suspended simply from taffeta ribbon finished with a *choux* or rosette.

Contemporary fabrics can be used to improvise the timeless style of traditional furnishings. The texture and Elizabethan quality of this acanthus-printed linen union creates an illusion of tapestry, while the ivory cotton chair upholstery suggests Georgian woven silk damask.

Urban Style

Urban style is characterized by a bold approach. While the colour palette remains cool and contemporary, and pattern is restrained to two complementary prints, the effect is unquestionably striking.

In an unmistakably urban setting it is often more effective to follow the pace of your surroundings and create a drawing room in a contemporary urban style. The look does not always imply high-tech chrome and glass, or minimalist severity. Comfort and elegance are still the priority, but here they are conveyed by a feeling of uncluttered space and natural light. Urban style has a pared-down sophistic-

ation evoked by simple, subtle decoration that lets the structural mood of the room speak for itself, whether it is a period town house, modern apartment, wharf or warehouse conversion.

Creating the Style

Colour Beside an abundance of daylight, the character of urban style is set by a contemporary colour scheme. The palette can either be decidedly neutral and understated, revolving round one master colour of ivory, sand or taupe; or cool and crisp in tones of pale apricot and grey, or duck-egg blue with beige. The key colours may be subdued but the treatment is always bold, incorporating expanses of plain colour on walls and windows to instate an atmosphere of ordered balance.

Pattern This is an equally important element. Simple geometrics, classic shirt or broad stripes, large-scale stylized florals and sprigs have a suitably abstract quality. Pattern can be used as a secondary element to introduce on chair and sofa covers, cushions and tablecloths. But one of the features of urban style is an economy of pattern: either restricting a scheme to one striking print, or using unobtrusive, related patterns to extend variety and texture to the master colour.

Walls and Windows

Curtains and Blinds Window treatment is understated, yet provides a luxuriant air. Quantities of plain smooth chintz hung from wooden poles, or an airy printed voile draped in a grand manner, give an unexpectedly modern twist. Or as an option to curtains, roman blinds accentuate the geometrics of a window frame and cast maximum daylight into the contemporary drawing room.

Furniture and Furnishings

Furniture In an urban drawing room, furniture conveys a sense of ease, but one with a contemporary edge to it. Long, low level geometric sofas accentuate the linear proportions of the room, emphasized by a straight

valance and contrast piped upholstery. A certain sophistication comes from a blend of classical and modern: the combination of a gilded French *fauteuil* with a low glass table; or of a Georgian mahogany chair upholstered in a pale slubbed weave.

Furnishings Related shades of soft smoke blue, taupe or grey heighten the decorative sense of unity. Variations in fabric texture, mixing chintz, or grainy linens with diamond and ribbed weaves, give added interest. A toning rug or fabric throw draped across the sofa adds tangible comfort and softens the contours of the room.

A neutral background of buttermilk and sand provides a base for complementary shades and graphic pattern. Smoke blue adds substance to the scheme and gives a unity to the decorative elements. The geometric fretwork design used on the sofa covers is carried through to the wide border above the skirting, a Chinese inspiration that is reinforced by the folding screen striped with oriental images.

RIGHT The low striped sofas, glass table and geometric rug all heighten an overwhelming sense of space in this airy loft conversion.

Decorative objects play an eye-catching role: the curved silhouettes of wrought-iron candlesticks contrast with the multi-coloured book spines below.

Floor and Fireplace

Polished Floorboards Parquet flooring or polished floorboards establish a contemporary mood in the urban drawing room, overlaid with a striking kelim or abstract patterned cotton rugs in cool colours. Vinyl tiles now simulate a parquet look too. Or the boards could be stencilled with a geometric pattern that conjures the look of elegant marquetry.

Fireplace This is an important focal point, even when purely decorative. A slate grey marble fire surround with its abstract grain bridges tradition with contemporary style. An uncluttered mantelpiece could be decorated with an asymmetrical arrangement of ornaments or statues.

Lighting

Subtle lighting is needed to counteract any stark decorative effects. Down lighting diffused from wall brackets can wash walls with light, complemented by tall column lamps with plain fabric shades. Or a low wattage spherical globe could cast floor level light, adding a touch of originality to the lighting scheme.

Decorative Details

Pictures bring a bold touch to the urban drawing room. However disparate their subject matter, they look more effective hung in a well ordered arrangement of similar size and shape: perhaps vertically paired or hung horizontally in a low straight line above the sofa. Prints or enlarged photographs can look as striking as original art, framed in simple perspex, grouped on one wall for an impact of colour and pattern.

A modern sculpture or more classical plaster bust, doubling as a hat stand, adds individuality and humour to the room. Furniture can also supply decorative distractions: a low chequerboard table could stand poised for a game of draughts or chess. But however urban the mood, fresh flowers are essential. An abundance of one species in a single colour has a contemporary style about it. Consider an array of lilies or tulips in tall glass vases, a jug of pale yellow roses or baskets brimming with white azaleas.

THE SITTING ROOM

Today the sitting room is traditionally less imposing than the drawing room, although as the main reception room in a house it fulfills the same functions. Whilst still smart it is usually a less formal room, smaller in size and furnished with generous sofas and chairs that invite hours of recreation.

The informal nature of a sitting room is reflected in its origins, evolving from the ladies' dressing room or boudoir where the mistress of the house entertained select company away from formal rules of etiquette. Although a private room, it was very much on show, decorated with a view to being admired, particularly in France where Madame Récamier's Empire-style boudoir was an inspiration to the fashion conscious.

In time, the ladies' sitting room moved downstairs and merged its role with the parlour, traditionally located on the ground floor at the back of the house and removed from the sequence of elaborate reception rooms above. The idea of a parlour is an anachronism today, recalling the high Victorian tradition of the late nineteenth century when the room acquired an almost sacred status. However humble the household, the parlour remained the best room used only on Sundays and special occasions. It contained only the smartest furniture – the ubiquitous parlour suite, the piano and most prized china, ornaments and photographs.

But the concept of the parlour as it was used in Tudor times has a certain relevance today, especially in a large house where a small, informal room is welcomed for its comfort, warmth and manageable proportions. The Tudor parlour was a relatively intimate room, warmed by oak panelling and tapestry hangings, which provided a retreat from communal life in the Great Hall, where the master and family could sit and dine apart from the crowded household. Some parlours contained beds, but their chief role was that of an informal dining room – a function that carried on into the eighteenth century when a quest for privacy away from servants and ritual formality set a precedent for small parties.

This relaxed and unpretentious atmosphere has evolved over centuries in answer to a perennial need for a haven of comfort and seclusion away from the pressures of everyday life. Decoration provides the key in recreating this ambience in sitting rooms today. The style you choose will be influenced by the period and scale of your room. Ideas drawn from

English country-house style conjure elegance on a cosy scale, while a rustic ambience is more suitable for cottage proportions. Or consider a wayward Bohemian scheme for a rambling, artistic room or an urban contemporary setting.

Choosing a Style to Suit the Room

The style of decoration must depend to a certain extent on the role and nature of the sitting room. Whether it is to be a setting for intimate entertaining, or an informal retreat for browsing through the morning newspapers, the priority is to create an atmosphere of warmth and comfort.

It is a room that can take a cheerful, imaginative decoration – not that the style should be imposing, but anything too tame or low key can feel lifeless and unwelcoming. On the other hand, if the decoration is too smart it may detract from the relaxed informality of a room where simple exuberance catches the romantic spirit. A certain shabbiness helps tone down an over-decorated look, but the preference for a relaxed atmosphere does not mean haphazard decoration, or cutting corners: the lived-in look evolves from a well-designed framework.

Creating the Style

Whatever the size and style of the room, a sense of unity created by clever use of colour, pattern and texture draws the whole together. The rapport between walls, curtains, furnishings and accessories can be played up or down to give different effects. But to give a room

character there needs to be some thread linking the overall scheme.

Colour Schemes Colour is an obvious and necessary link that sets the mood of a sitting room. The number of colours involved as well as the actual shades are key factors. Minimal schemes restricted to one or two neutral or understated pastel tones create a sophisticated, uncluttered atmosphere. A palette of three or four colours that lets incidental shades creep in – with essential cushions, lamps, books and pictures – feels more homely and informal. In each scheme the dominant colour is combined with a secondary palette in contrast to or a variation of the master colour. Sitting-room colours need to evoke warmth and light. Yellow has a timeless, cheering quality that suits rooms of all sizes and helps conjure sunshine in midwinter. Shades of coral with terracotta are instantly warming and give a secure glow to a room. Colour groups of similar tone are easy to live with, especially with an element of white that lifts the scheme. Deeper tones of dark green, burgundy, crimson or navy introduce an air of permanence and tradition, while pale colours like duck-egg blue, shell pink, cowslip yellow and buttermilk have a luminous clarity that is refreshing and peaceful to live with.

Fabrics The essential warmth of a sitting

room is emphasized by its fabrics. A classic floral chintz has just the right balance of cosy elegance for a sitting room in the town or country – especially a bold cabbage rose design in cowslip yellow or rose pink, entwined with apple green leaves. Satin-weave cotton and linen union also belong in a sitting room. They blend naturally together and acquire a faded charm that gives a sense of permanence to the room. Fabrics can be chosen to reinforce the mood of an historical period. Linen printed with a traditional flamestitch design has Elizabethan overtones; jewel-coloured cotton sateen, printed with garlands, birds, fruit and flowers conjures a cosy Victorian ladies' sitting room.

Pattern Sitting-room furnishings offer great scope for a variety of patterns and textures. Using print and fabric in generous quantities gives the room an instinctive air of comfort and luxury. Pattern is part of the charm of the sitting room and a necessary way to dilute blocks of colour. Where two or three prints

feature in a room, a restful effect comes from letting one dominate. The companion prints should be related colourwise, but there is no need to carry through a diminutive thread of the master pattern. A bold floral design on the curtains can combine with a gentle stripe or trellis wallpaper, and a small check pattern in the upholstery and accessories. In reverse, a bold Regency stripe can be enhanced by a quiet floral, small geometric or abstract print. A paper border around the walls is a useful link between curtain and wall design.

Where the pattern is used also determines its effect on the room. A bold print applied to the walls will dominate a room, whereas the same print used in the curtains will be less insistent, even less so on the upholstery or loose covers where it will merge with diverse cushions, rugs and objects in the room. An onslaught of pattern can be tiring to live with. Where curtains are a strong feature of a room, it is often more striking to paint the walls a complementary colour, rather than using a contrasting or toning pattern.

ABOVE *This full-blown Victorian design of English cabbage roses gives an air of settled tradition in true country-house style. The coral-pink piping of the curtain tie-backs links the colour and stripe in the wallpaper, while the panelled dado echoes the fine trellis ground of the fabric and adds a neutral quality to the scheme.*

LEFT *Colour has a potent effect on the atmosphere in a room. Here a bold yellow scheme conjures a cheerful, sunny mood and unifies the pattern of the wallpaper, upholstery and bright needlepoint rugs. The substantial sofa and armchairs instate an irresistible air of relaxed comfort.*

RIGHT *A border adds definition to the symmetry and architectural proportions of a room. This bold pattern following the contours of the door frame and dado rail reflects the discreet woven stripe in the pale wallpaper. The original pairing of sand and rich lavender blue evokes a Georgian calm, sharpened with crisp white paintwork.*

ABOVE *Late Victorian walls succumbed to elaborate polychromatic treatment. The wide floral frieze bordering the doorway and skirting echoes the swagged ribbons below the painted cornice. The jade-green grained door with its lily-painted panels suggest a faintly oriental air, played up by the chinoiserie plates above.*

Walls and Windows

Paint Finishes The walls in a sitting room are more than a question of paper or paintwork. While essentially a restful background to the room, they still deserve original treatment. Instead of a flat coat of standard emulsion, a decorative finish can be applied that gives interest without an obvious pattern. The revival of ragging, sponging and dragging suits the informality of a sitting room, giving depth and texture to a single overall colour. For a rustic effect, conjure a traditional cottage pink with a diluted terracotta glaze sponged onto white walls. A mellow pinkish brick fireplace surround could be allied to the walls by sponging warm ochre over a pale coral background.

Tent Room For a more sophisticated look create an intimate cocoon with walls and curtains in the same bold colour and pattern to provide solace on dull, grey days. Extending the pattern over the ceiling as well intensifies the effect and recalls a tent room of the late eighteenth century, where fabric was draped from the ceiling like the inside of a tent. The same idea can be interpreted today with fabric or wallpaper. With wallpaper, the intensity of pattern can be alleviated by contrasting pain-twork at the cornice, or a border applied below the ceiling. For a fabric tent, chintz or satin-weave cotton are suitably soft materials to drape in a tented effect. The pattern can be of delicate florals for a romantic arbour, or of bolder paisleys that conjure an air of oriental mystique.

Wallpaper Borders These can add style and polish to a wall. They are also useful devices for defining the architectural structure and giving proportion to a room. A tall ceiling can be lowered with a border below the cornice or

just under the ceiling and above the skirting board – an effect which condenses the wall space. For continuity through the room a border can be extended around door frames, windows and fireplace surrounds, or used to frame real or *trompe-l'oeil* wall panelling.

Curtains Sitting-room windows benefit from a romantic treatment to accentuate an intimate atmosphere. Curtains need to be generous enough to enclose the room. Wherever practically possible, floor-length rather than sill-length curtains add a dimension of comfort, especially when interlined and weighted to rest on the ground. They also add a sense of height to a low-ceilinged room.

Pelmet A well-chosen pelmet contributes to the whole effect, enhancing the windows and turning the curtains into a key feature of the room, by day as well as by night. The style of pelmet depends on the window shape, the texture of the curtain material and the outlook itself. There is little point having an elaborate pelmet if it is going to compete with an overpowering view. A simple gathered pelmet with a self frill or tasselled fringe may be appropriate to a less imposing situation. If a pelmet obscures too much light at a small window, an answer is to hang the curtains on a plain brass or wooden pole with a decorative finial at each end – pineapples were a popular eighteenth-century motif – or to mask the curtain rod with a Victorian bell-pull.

There is no reason to give smaller windows modest treatment, provided they are not dwarfed by ornate pelmets. Full-length curtains lend importance to the windows and provide space for a more grandiose pattern that would otherwise look unbalanced on sill-length curtains. Hanging curtains on a wider pole, set well above the window, maximizes the amount of natural light coming into the room and also gives a larger area to display the fabric when the curtains are drawn.

Lining The curtain lining does not have to be standard white or cream. A stronger colour that echoes the master pattern adds density to the finished curtains.

Decorative Trims The pelmet trim can be repeated on the hem or down the edges of the curtains. Tie-backs make essential decorative details that give a definite daytime shape to the curtains. They can be of matching material, stiffened and bound with a co-ordinating colour, or of silken twisted cord with tassel or pommel ends.

Blinds These are an option to use alone or combine with curtains. A festoon blind in chintz or cotton has a femininity that can be played up with a flounced frill or tasselled edging. A fine cotton roller blind hung between the curtains and the window is both decorative and practical, as it can be pulled down to filter strong sunlight. A gathered panel of fine lace or voile introduces a romantic touch to the window, softening sharp contours while retaining the architectural outline of the frame. Such delicate fabrics can be used alone for a fresh simple outlook: a fine panel of lace or taffeta can be ruched into a

A romantic window corner with an air of tranquillity emanates from this Victorian scheme of plum and taupe that captures the characteristic interplay of rich texture, pattern and trimmings. The sweeping tasselled curtains have an underplayed flamboyance with a chintz lining that matches the hollyhock wallpaper.

RIGHT *A sitting room furnished with a view to both comfort and practicality, well equipped for hours of relaxation and the necessary pleasures of afternoon tea beside the fire. This grand-scale blend of coral stripes and bold cabbage roses instates a timeless serenity, enhanced by the spacious proportions of the room. These are elegantly defined by the rosy swag border, sage-green dado and picture rail.*

ABOVE *An abundance of soft cushions increases the sense of cosiness in a sitting room, adding plain fabrics and companion prints to the master pattern.*

festooned Austrian blind, a sheer veil of muslin or tulle tumbled over the curtain rods could fall as detached elements of the curtain lining, or a gentle fall of voile could be draped across the window as an asymmetrical curtain. A simple but effective treatment that conjures hot climates consists of a length of flimsy white cotton, looped over a curtain rod to create a soft swagged pelmet above an un-curtained window.

Furniture and Furnishings

Organization The arrangement of furniture in a room has a crucial effect on the whole ambience. The practicalities of comfort count at a basic level: how the chairs are positioned and whether they can 'talk' naturally to one another; whether the room is well lit for reading, with switches within easy reach and convenient tables for putting down books or a drink; and whether draughty corners are shielded by cleverly positioned furniture, or a fabric screen.

Furniture Style The sitting room is the place for smaller, lightweight pieces: a classic two-seater sofa covered in a sunny chintz or wickerwork cotton; for Regency painted chairs with cane seats; a buttoned slipper chair upholstered in fruit-printed chintz; a footstool or ottoman. In a small space, a co-ordinating suite of sofa and chairs adds unity and cosiness, while a larger room can carry off a more eclectic accumulation of sofas and chairs. Furniture need not be scaled down to fit the room: a generous sofa can extend along the length of one wall, almost as an inbuilt fixture.

Furniture must be comfortable. Squared solid shapes present a traditional atmosphere, while the rounded curves of ottomans, *chaises duchesses*, slipper chairs and footstools create more of a boudoir effect.

Round occasional tables are the perfect frame for an elegant draped cloth, which can be linked to the overall mood of the room with trimmings: contrast binding or webbing gives a neat look in a co-ordinating colour, while a deep fringe or ruffle is a softer finish.

Furnishings Whether as a matching set or not, the loose covers or upholstery should relate to the whole scheme of the room, echoing the colour and pattern of the curtains and walls. Plain covers, perhaps with a contrast piping that picks out another colour in the room, are always a reliable choice and make a backdrop for interesting cushions of tapestry, patchwork, chintz or brocade that add character to the room. A classic linen union or slub cotton adds texture to plain covers without a definite pattern. Avoid a uniform look with an assortment of shapes and

A squared substantial armchair with its geometric contours sharpened by a trellis-patterned loose cover, contrast piping and crisp box-pleated valance.

A traditional upright armchair is smartened with a sophisticated fringed valance that echoes its striped upholstery.

A voluptuous armchair exuding deep sprung comfort recalls the settled ease of an Edwardian sitting room.

A classic Georgian wing armchair with scrolled arms is covered in rosy chintz with a deep ruffled valance.

An extravagant effect for a table cloth, where a secondary fabric is draped into a ribbon tie around the floral table cloth.

A romantic boudoir touch with a swagged hemline looped up into place by contrasting rosettes.

hair oil from staining the upholstery, can take the form of a tartan travel rug, a paisley shawl or the traditional starched, embroidered linens draped across the back of sofas and chairs.

Floor and Fireplace

Floor This is an area that sustains the warm and sunny atmosphere of a sitting room. Natural floor boards, a pale looped pile carpet or closely woven matting are all infallible backgrounds. The soft shade of fawn that John Fowler christened 'mouse's back' is a natural foil for an assortment of rugs, whether Indian wool dhurries, oriental kelims or home-stitched needlepoint rugs beside the hearth. Alternatively a printed Brussels weave carpet with its looped pile has a crisp needlepoint texture that gives the room a Victorian quality. A large expanse of dark carpet or rug steals too much precious light; colours are best kept soft and muted to reflect without dominating the overall scheme.

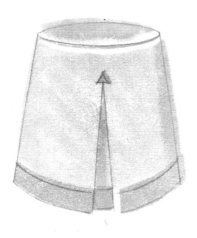

A sleek, tailored effect, created by a stiffened fabric tablecloth with an inverted pleat, contrasting border and piped rim.

Classic Victorian style is recalled by draping a lace cloth over plain velvet or satin weave cotton.

Fireplace In a sitting room the fireplace is less imposing than the ornate carved marble of the drawing room and built more for warmth and comfort than to impress. It is a luxury today that was taken for granted in the last century, when it would have been dutifully cleaned out and relit before breakfast, with its brass fender polished daily. A hearth or fire surround patterned with a patchwork of faded antique or blue-and-white delft tiles adds a period quality that is appropriately cosy and informal. In summer, fill an unlit grate with an arrangement of fresh flowers or evergreens. A tradition of the American settlers was to fill the grate with pine boughs and fircones giving an aromatic scent to the room. The mantelpiece is a perfect ledge for a collection of Stafford-shire figures and flowers in pretty china vases.

RIGHT *A garland of roses on a warm hearth rug extends an inviting touch to the fireplace, with a soft pile texture in gentle contrast to the carved fire surround and curly brass fender. A mantelpiece display sets a mood of cultured elegance endorsed by the candelabra and Victorian seascapes.*

sizes for the cushions; some round, rectangular or square with piped, frilled or fringed edges. Romantic touches can be added with a frilled or ruffled valance on a floral chintz loose cover.

The look of comfort is just as vital as the feel of it. Loose covers should be an ample, generous fit, with plenty of give, and a valance that rests on the carpet. Antimacassars, invented by the Victorians to prevent men's black macassar

Lighting

To a great extent, lighting controls the ambience of a sitting room. Table lamps or wall brackets have a much more gentle effect than overhead lighting.

Positioning the lighting is a crucial and difficult decision that often has to be made at the planning stage of a room. Table lamps are more versatile, but to look effective they need to be on a generous scale. Both lamp base and shade are decorative as well as functional elements: the taller the base, the more efficient the spread of light. A classic vase or column-shaped base in ceramic or wood combines well with a simple conical or pleated fabric shade, which can be trimmed with braid or a tasselled fringe to link with the furnishings, cushions or pelmet.

A mirror above a fireplace increases the sense of space in a small room and adds light and elegance to the walls, particularly if it is placed opposite a window to reflect the light.

A contemporary 'garniture' of blue and white china brings a homely touch into the room. The soft mottled blues relate to the delicate stencilled bouquets, the painted door surround and finely striped wallpaper.

Decorative Details

A memorable sitting room is one with surprising pockets of interest: a corner cupboard, shelved alcove or recess arranged with books, china and photographs that add character without cluttering the atmosphere.

China Grouped china plates on the walls, arrayed along a projecting cornice or picture rail in a seventeenth-century style, or alternatively displayed above the door frame or fireplace create an attractive effect. Decorative arrangements of uneven numbered sets of porcelain or ornaments known as a 'garniture' were typical of the eighteenth century. Victorians were great collectors of oriental porcelain, and filled any bare wall space or alcove with a display. Chinoiserie porcelain vases and decorative tea sets look attractive in today's sitting room, especially blue and white set against a yellow backdrop.

Flowers A profusion of fresh flowers brings the country indoors and fills the sitting room with irresistible scent and colour. It is the most unpretentious kind of luxury and has a magnetic effect on the atmosphere. To feed the sense of smell is as important as sight and touch in a room. Bowls of pot-pourri, redolent of lavender, roses, herbs and spices give lasting fragrance through the grey winter months, as does a clove-scented Elizabethan pommander hanging from a ribbon beside the fireplace, but few things can rival the evocative fragrance of old-fashioned roses, sweetpeas, hyacinths or lilies-of-the-valley in their season. Flowers are a natural way to enhance the colour scheme in a sitting room, or introduce brilliance to a pastel scheme.

Pictures are an essential element that can transform a room, often adding an indefinable

A print room of Etruscan influence, inspired by the Classical Revival of the Regency period. Prints derived from Greek vase decoration are pasted in tiers directly onto the terracotta-washed wall. The fireplace is genuine, but the dentil moulded cornice, picture ribbons and panelling are obviously trompe-l'oeil.

quality that gives life and a highly personal touch. The sitting room provides an ideal setting for a collection of miniatures grouped informally together, or botanical fruit and flower prints in simple gilt frames. A charming eighteenth-century fashion was to suspend one or a tier of pictures on a wide ribbon, gimp or strip of taffeta, decorating the group with a bow or rosette at the top, or above each frame. These could be sewn from the curtain fabric, or perhaps a toning print.

The picture grouping may appear slightly random, but there has to be a balance and order between them all to create a successful effect. The informality can be emphasized by putting the pictures in different frames — ideally those that have some affinity with each other — to create an elegant assortment of distressed gilt, painted wood or lacquer. Victorians grouped their oils, watercolours, prints and mezzotints in informal tiers, two or three pictures deep. The pictures themselves can be of assorted shape and size, with oval or round frames among squares or rectangles.

Creating a Print Room The idea of a print room could be incorporated into wall decoration. It was an eighteenth-century style invented by Lord Cardigan for displaying prints acquired on the Grand Tour, pasting them directly onto the walls. Each print was framed by a delicate engraved border, and linked by festooned garlands. The fashion spread among country houses and was especially popular in ladies' sitting rooms where the prints were set against a straw yellow or pale pink moiré wallpaper. Today, delicate stencilling of frame-like borders could be applied around a *trompe-l'oeil* picture mural or print to recreate a contemporary print room.

RIGHT *Clear, sunny colours evoke a refreshing country ambience and increase the sense of space in a room. Simple folkloric patterns blend naturally together, underlining a rustic charm.*

BELOW *The underplayed look of sill-length curtains, hung from a narrow wooden pole, embodies the rustic spirit. Their leafy design reflects the stencilled walls and unifies the country tones of antique wood, straw and rush matting.*

A Rustic Idyll

This style of sitting room plays up the romantic idyll of cottage life. Irregularity is a decorative feature, accentuated by unevenly proportioned rooms with low ceiling beams, bay windows and inglenook fireplaces. The decoration has a simple settled look, epitomized by mellow patchwork cushions, rag rugs, samplers and fresh cottage flowers. Nothing looks new or contrived. Walls are plaster pink or whitewashed, enhanced by rustic stencilling. Fabrics are sprigged cottage cottons or faded chintzes, aged where necessary in a bath of tea for a timewashed look.

Creating the Style

Colour and Pattern Rustic style has a simplicity that comes from a closely related colour scheme: a palette in faded country hues of old-fashioned pinks, coral, sand, pale sage and smoke blue that recall natural vegetable dyes. Pattern is a characteristic part of the room, typified by gentle florals and cottage sprigs – although a larger sitting room is enhanced by bolder poppies, cornflowers and dandelions or clusters of pansies strewn across cottons and chintzes.

While unmistakably comfortable, this sitting room has an honest humble charm, emphasized by its eclectic furnishings. Old friendly sofas and armchairs, salvaged from attics, auctions and junk shops, are overhauled and re-covered in faded linen union or muted cotton prints, then given extra padding with tartan rugs and home-sewn patchwork cushions. The floor accentuates the rustic atmosphere with bare wooden boards or jute matting clad with rag or tapestried rugs.

Walls and Windows

Paint and Paper As cottage windows tend to be small, sitting-room walls need to convey a feeling of light. Where pure white appears too stark, a tinge of sand, coral or pale sage can diffuse the glare, giving a subtle glow to the walls. A frieze or skirting stencilled with a rambling rose or flower posy adds homespun detail to the paintwork – an idea that can continue over wooden furniture, doors or mantelshelf. Paint is an effective cover on uneven, beamed walls, but in a modern or urban setting a rustic wallpaper can infuse the room with a more rural atmosphere – especially if it extends over the ceiling or behind shelves and alcoves. Traditional cottage prints are stippled and sprigged on a cream background, giving surface interest without specific pattern.

Curtains and Pelmets Windows need a simple touch, with unadorned cotton or chintz to frame a rural outlook or conjure the countryside in a town setting. Pelmets need be no more than a ruffle to hide the curtain rail. At a small window, or where French windows lead onto a garden or balcony, consider hanging only one curtain, tied back with a matching bow. In summer when curtains are more decorative than practical, cotton lace makes an original alternative to an opaque fabric, whether hung as a single panel or gathered into a pair of simple curtains.

Furniture and Furnishings

The idiosyncratic furnishings of a rustic sitting room emphasize its air of homely comfort. A wicker sofa, plump with cotton cushions, is draped with a fading patchwork comforter; rush-seated Windsor chairs, a rocker and upright settle are softened with bolsters and

squab cushions. An old pine dresser is arrayed with decorative china; teapots, jugs, cups, photographs, plants and bunches of cottage flowers. New wood could be given a time-worn patina of greyish blue or sage green with a milky paint finish rubbed into the grain.

Furnishing Fabrics While the furnishing fabrics seldom match, the mellow pastel shades, the sprigged and stippled prints all have a natural affinity that infuses the room with a pastoral tranquility. The peasant tradition introduces splashes of warm colour and pattern; naive lattice and floral prints come in cinnamon, paprika, emerald and scarlet, inspired by East European embroideries and folkloric costume.

A scheme of sweet-pea pastels fills a room with a pastoral calm. The background paper of climbing flowers entwined along a trellis border supplies a colour spectrum of lavender, sapphire, rose pink and jade for the surrounding decoration. Here, simplicity dominates, with crisp striped curtains below a scalloped pelmet, neutral upholstery softened with sprigged cushions and quilts, and timeworn antique furniture.

Lighting

Simplicity extends to the style of lighting which needs to evoke a low-tech ambience. Hand-carved wooden or wrought metal wall brackets, or table lamps adapted from unglazed terracotta urns could be backed up by light from beeswax candles burning in china candlesticks.

Decorative Details

Pictures with a hand-crafted quality are appropriate here, perhaps a tapestry or fabric collage of the countryside, or a child's sampler. Or decorate the walls with a collection of hand-painted plates or tiles, beautiful straw hats, baskets or embroidered shawls. Dried flowers and hops entwined into swags can festoon the walls or hang in bunches from ceiling hooks.

ABOVE *These large-scale stencilled leaves have a bold, free-hand quality that follows the sweeping curve and carving of the staircase. Keeping the pattern to closely related colours complements the natural grain of the floorboards.*

RIGHT *Candlelight cast from a simple shaded wall sconce adds a soft, low-tech glow to the atmosphere.*

FAR RIGHT *The fireplace assumes a decorative, as well as a functional focus, painted with a pastoral scene in colours that reflect the fresh, simple interior. A wicker basket of lavender fills the open hearth.*

Floor and Fireplace

Floorboards or Matting Well scrubbed floorboards are warmed with cheerful rag rugs of assorted size and shape, or covered with honey-coloured sisal matting. For a decorative effect, exposed boards could be stencilled with a rambling floral pattern round the edge of the room.

Fireplace With furniture grouped around the hearth, a fireplace becomes the focal point of a rustic sitting room. It needs only a simple treatment, its wooden fire surround and mantelpiece waxed or rubbed with a tinge of colour to echo the dresser or other painted furniture. Draughts from the open bricked hearth could be shielded by a *trompe l'oeil* chimney board depicting a landscape or naive animal painting.

RIGHT
Exuberant Bloomsbury style is tempered by a calm colour palette and artful balance of patterns. This sitting room has a spontaneous, relaxed quality evoked by comfortably cushioned armchairs and homely evidence of day-to-day living.

ABOVE *Bloomsbury-style paintwork has an inventive spirit enriching mouldings, panelling and walls with unconstrained pattern.*

The Bohemian Sitting Room

The Bloomsbury style of the 1930s is an artistic expression of the vernacular, with a free spirited approach that suits the informality of the sitting room. The foundation of this distinctive decoration was created by Vanessa Bell and Duncan Grant at Charleston, a rambling farmhouse in Sussex that became the focus of the Bloomsbury movement.

The style is characterized by its painterly qualities: its spontaneous profusion of bold, primitive pattern that spills over walls, curtains, rugs, floorboards and furniture, as if every available surface is a blank canvas awaiting decoration. In a Bloomsbury room, even patterned radiators form part of the interior scheme. The characteristic motifs of nudes, dancers, fruit bowls, flowers and abstract geometrics have an eccentric charm, emphasized by the startling colour combinations.

Creating the Style

Colour The exuberance of Bloomsbury pattern needs to be tempered by a more tranquil approach to colour. A contemporary palette of intense pastels − rose pink, apricot, straw yellow, aquamarine and jade − provides a unified backdrop to the abstract spirit of the sitting room. The artistic effect can be played up or down: pairing grey with pink or yellow for a sophisticated restraint, or incorporating all the shades for an unabashed éclat of pattern and colour. An element of white on fabric or paintwork adds an immediate vitality, while stronger accents of dark green or plum give depth to the scheme.

Paint The key to the style is giving an innovative air to the room: a mood set by hand-painted decoration, embellishing doors, screens, lamp bases and shades, ceramics, a tiled fire surround, even a wooden log box.

Walls and Windows

Paint and Paper Wall decoration is an integral feature of the style that needs to blend in without dominating the inevitable array of pictures that jostle for space. The soothing grey and white backdrop of stars and daisies stencilled in the sitting room at Charleston could be recreated with paintwork and stencils or suggested by a stippled wallpaper.

ABOVE *A simple deep-set window is given artistic impact by an extravagant painted mural. The figurative vases and* trompe-l'oeil *row of plates contrast happily with the diffuse pattern sponged over the walls.*

LEFT *Walls papered with cream daisies on a straw ground harmonize with this theatrical window treatment, where abstract floral curtains contrast with a bold pelmet and tie-backs that have a hand-painted look about them.*

Curtains and Pelmets Windows can provide a more striking source of decoration. A grainy linen union scattered with abstract florals has a bold hand-painted finish that suits the scale of a large window. Consider adding a deep gathered pelmet and tie-backs in a colour or print variation of the master pattern, giving an unexpected flourish to the outlook. A window-seat could continue the scheme, with a banquette covered to match the curtains and a valance that repeats the pelmet design.

Furniture and Furnishings

The Bohemian sitting room has a lived-in vitality, emphasized by its comfortable furni-

RIGHT *A sitting room with an authentic hand-painted look, created by Vanessa Bell's granddaughter Cressida Bell. Striped walls supply a muted base for a plethora of softly coloured abstract pattern, giving an effect of comfortable disarray to the generously proportioned sofa.*

FAR RIGHT ABOVE *Run a strong thread of continuity through a room by linking a ceramic lamp base and fabric shade to an abstract cushion cover, and a tablecloth to an archetypal Bloomsbury cushion.*

FAR RIGHT BELOW *Hand-painted ceramics, interpreting classic Bloomsbury design, add a further dimension of pattern and texture to the Bohemian theme.*

ture covered in a carefree mix of colour and pattern. Deep-seated armchairs set beside the fireplace have generous loose covers in plain linen union to offset their patterned cushions and drapes. A small sofa, clad in printed cotton, has a full gathered valance and bank of contrasting cushions and bolsters, while upholstered footstools and covered tables, positioned for books, wineglasses, plants and reading lamps, accentuate the Bohemian atmosphere.

Floor and Fireplace

Carpets and Rugs A large Turkish carpet, its colours muted by sunlight, will add another dimension to the bold play of pattern. Used wall-to-wall, it will maintain an aura of comfort and increase the sense of space in a small room. Alternatively, a wool rug in a bold Omega design will highlight the artistic theme.

Fireplace This could be understated, either left as an unpretentious wooden surround or incorporated into the scheme with a coat of gloss paint that blends with the key colours in the room. Or think of it as a blank canvas awaiting decoration with Bloomsbury-style dancers, fruit bowls, flowers or geometrics – a design that could extend to hand painted tiles on the hearth. The mantelpiece provides a focus for colour and pattern with exuberant geraniums trailing from terracotta pots.

Lighting

The artistic mood continues. Gentle low-level lighting is provided by pottery lamp bases, painted with abstract patterns and paired with corresponding painted fabric shades. A Thirties mood could be carried through with an authentic frosted glass pendant lamp, dis-

covered in an attic corner or a country antique shop.

Decorative Details

A random arrangement of books, ceramics, postcards and photographs arranged in haphazard fashion on simple painted wooden shelves brings out the personal quality of the Bohemian sitting room. Voluptuous bunches of stocks, hydrangeas and old fashioned roses add a breath of fresh air to the setting.

French windows help to make this room a perfect niche to catch the morning sun that filters through luxurious floral chintz curtains.

The Sitting Room as Morning Room

The morning room appeared at the end of the eighteenth century as a female counterpart to the library. It was traditionally a small, intimate and sunlit room where the mistress of the household could spend her morning atten-ding to domestic accounts, servants' duties, letter-writing and needlework. Where no breakfast parlour existed the morning room provided a light, sunny place to take breakfast. As Mrs Peel, a professional decorator, advised in the *New Home* magazine in 1898: 'Where that terrible meal the English breakfast pre-vails, we need all the cheering which we can possibly receive in the early hours of the morning.'

Whether as a setting for breakfast or as a place to start the day browsing through newspapers, the idea of a morning room has an air of nostalgic comfort and civilization about it. It brings to mind the image of a room scented with flowers and freshly ground coffee, bathed in pale morning sunlight, with large sash or French windows leading to the garden or conservatory.

The morning room was originally on the ground floor, often as an informal annexe beside the drawing room. Today the concept of light, sunny decoration can be applied to any appropriate room in the house, apartment or cottage that faces south or east to catch the morning light. An upstairs spare bedroom could be used, with a balcony as a substitute for ground-floor access to the garden. Or it need not be a room at all: an upstairs hallway that catches the morning light could be turned into a peaceful niche with a comfortable window-seat, or armchair and table set permanently into an undisturbed recess.

Creating the Style

Colour First impressions in a morning room should be of gentle luminous colour, of fresh pattern and soft fabrics. Conjure an English garden with a sweet pea palette of rose pink, sapphire blue and jade, or the translucence of an early sky with duck-egg blue brightened by touches of emerald or crushed strawberry. For a Mediterranean glow, think of warm apricot and taupe, spiced with coral, terracotta and sage. A palette of yellow, from buttermilk to brilliant cowslip, creates a sunny mood on the dullest day. The play of light and shadow in a morning room adds an unexpected brightness to a subtle base colour like pale sand, ivory or pale sage, instating a calm order to the atmosphere.

Using only one colour creates a strong impact, especially in a small room. Alternatively, there is a place for a careful balance of bright colours. The brilliance of sapphire blue, emerald and scarlet against white recalls the freshness of a Swedish country interior depicted by the nineteenth-century artist Carl Larsson. Or borrow artistic inspiration from Monet's house at Giverny, near Paris; with a painter's eye for colour, the brilliance of mustard yellow and sky blue are combined to dazzling effect.

Walls and Windows

Wallpaper The walls in a morning room should have a strong rapport with the windows. The effect of simple curtains or pelmets can be echoed by very plain wall decoration. Where curtains are more flamboyant, wallpaper can continue the pattern and colour, or introduce a secondary print. Look at the background of curtain fabric for ideas. A fine stipple, scumble or trellis pattern behind a bold floral design can be repeated on the walls, using a corresponding paper or paint finish to match the effect.

This early-nineteenth-century chintz of lilies and carnations on a pale scumbled ground sums up the lady-like nature of a morning room. The matching border unifies the scheme, linking the wickerwork trellis wallpaper to the delicate floral design.

Skilful butter-yellow paintwork gives an impression of classical mouldings above a faux *marbled dado, an effect intensified by a genuine marble fireplace, classical ornament and pictures. The gilded glass overmantel adds a sense of light and space to the scene.*

Paint and Borders Wall treatment should be decorative without appearing too complicated. Instead of a paper border to add emphasis, consider using grosgrain ribbon or herringbone gimp to trim the meeting point of ceiling and wallpaper. Architectural features can be played up with white paintwork, possibly tinged with the key colour of the room. In a tall, light setting a tinted ceiling gives a subtle dimension of colour. There was a fashion for pale green or grey in the early nineteenth century, with the cornice painted in a similar – but darker – shade.

Painted Panelling This was a feature of small Georgian living rooms, where as a change from graining, cheap pine panelling was painted in a vivid duck-egg blue, jade green or butter yellow. The idea could be used in a morning room, painting or creating *faux* panelling to cover an entire wall, or from skirting to dado height. A floral wallpaper that resembles chintz or a Chinese silk hanging could be applied above, with a dado-level border linking the two schemes. A charming Swedish custom of the period was to cover walls with panels of canvas decorated with delicate flower garlands. A picture in a gilded frame was hung on each panel, suspended from a ribbon.

Windows With the importance of morning light and access to the garden, deep sash or French windows become a focal point of the room. Floor-length curtains make a romantic frame to the scenery beyond, an effect that should be bold, yet simple, with deep pleated or softly festooned pelmets. Where the room leads onto the garden, extra light could be let in through a glazed door. When positioned in a corner of the room, it is simpler to hang one full curtain to one side of the door that can be drawn across if the room is used at night. Thick padded or interlined curtains add essential insulation, as well as a feeling of underplayed extravagance.

Furniture and Furnishings

Play up the feminine origins of the morning room with delicate, ladylike furniture: an elegant bureau or writing table, Victorian button-back slipper chairs, a damask-covered *chaise-longue* for reclining with the newspapers, footstools and a small chintz sofa scattered with full-blown roses and flounced cushions. Related texture and pattern can be incorporated in the furnishings, combining country garden florals with striped, checked and stippled prints on smooth chintzes and satin weave cottons. An edging of braid, bullion fringe or tassels could smarten a tapestried footstool, table cloth or cushions.

Floor and Fireplace

Floor A pale fitted carpet or wall-to-wall rush matting brings an impression of natural light into the room. Both make a suitable background for a large floral rug or dhurrie patterned in pale sunlit colours.

Fireplace This could assume a Victorian mood, its contours softened by a feminine valance of swathed muslin or fringed chintz. Vases of fresh flowers are essential to the mantelpiece, while a gilded rococo mirror above the fireplace adds a touch of frivolity that also magnifies the morning light.

Lighting

Let the play of natural daylight and shadow become a decorative feature of the room. Artificial back-up lighting should be unobtrusive and well placed in the form of delicate wall brackets, small candelabra or table lamps, with bases adapted, perhaps, from an antique tin tea caddy.

Decorative Details

Although the drawing room was the correct place for afternoon tea, the morning room provided a less formal setting for an impromptu morning tea party. The eighteenth-century mood could be captured by a collection of accessories essential to the ritual: a Georgian fruitwood tea caddy, a kettle stand where a silver kettle would once have been warmed over a spirit lamp, round mahogany tea tables, trays of papier mâché or tôle ware, or a porcelain tea service displayed in a corner cupboard or alcove.

LEFT *A romantic touch of a gathered muslin valance along the mantelpiece softens the contours of a fireplace; an unconventional, decidedly feminine arrangement.*

BELOW *The translucence of an early morning sky is captured by this summery chintz. The upholstered Georgian armchair and draped table are poised by the uncurtained French windows which, when opened, joins the morning room and garden together.*

THE LIBRARY

A living room decorated in the style of a library has a feeling of relaxed comfort. Undisturbed by the noise and throng of the household, it has a settled, traditional air with shelves of books as a starting point for the decorative scheme, ready for browsing through from a deep, capacious armchair.

Originally, the library was a male bastion. In the sixteenth century, the gentleman's secret domain was his closet – a rarified room beyond the bedchamber where he would entertain close friends and conduct private business affairs. Under the French influence, an elaborately decorated closet became known as the *cabinet*, a place of safekeeping for a gentleman's most precious possessions: his writing desk, quills, maps, pictures and the few books he owned, stored in chests or arranged haphazardly on open compartments that lined the walls. Literacy and learning were not widely prized attributes for a sixteenth-century gentleman. But a fascination for the arts, scientific discovery and exploration during the seventeenth century inspired a quest for knowledge. Books became a symbol of culture and education that added to a man's prestige. As the closet shelves overflowed with books, a separate library became an essential feature of the eighteenth-century house, displaying collections of antiquities and pictures gathered on the Grand Tour.

As the library expanded, its role changed too, moving from an exclusive male sanctum into a family drawing room, its more comfortable surroundings created by the female members of the household. By the end of century the library had become an informal living room to occupy during the day. It was seldom hushed, but a room reflecting the Georgian zest for life, where a family and numerous guests could enjoy books of all kinds, explore maps of the New World or play card games, chess or backgammon.

Today a living room decorated in the style of a library assumes a general role rather than that of an exclusive place for reading and study. It can incorporate a working corner, but a feeling of relaxed comfort dominates more noticeably than any academic pursuits. The library living room is not just somewhere for peaceful contemplation, but also for entertaining, watching television and browsing through the books that furnish the room with a calm, reassuring atmosphere. As Sydney Smith, the nineteenth-century preacher, affirmed, 'There is no furniture so charming as books.'

RIGHT *A strong Gothic influence pervades this Victorian interior with its club-like colour scheme of crimson and sand and its antiquarian bookish atmosphere. The authentic Gothic throne and crenellated bookcase are set against characteristic geometric pattern on the walls, upholstery and Brussels weave carpet.*

Today a living room decorated in the style of a library assumes a general role rather than that of an exclusive place for reading and study. It can incorporate a working corner, but a feeling of relaxed comfort dominates more noticeably than any academic pursuits.

Choosing a Style to Suit the Room

BELOW *To fulfill its role as a family sitting room, this early-nineteenth-century library is furnished for studious and recreational pursuits. Decoration follows the country-house tradition with an imposing fireplace and dominant carved bookcases surmounted by family portraits and classical busts.*

Where a collection of books forms a starting point for a decorative scheme, follow the traditional atmosphere of a country-house library, or adopt a contemporary scheme where books provide a focus of colour and form. Besides books, a collection of pottery, porcelain, sculpture or fossils can look appropriate in such a setting, sympathetically displayed in bookcases or modern perspex cabinets across the wall.

As well as enhancing the content, a library style must also blend with the proportions and setting of your room. In a modern town house or flat where full-blown tradition can seem rather an anchronism, it is more effective to instate a contemporary mood. Classic library style could be given an unexpected modern twist with a surprisingly pale colour scheme and open-plan whitewashed bookshelves interspersed with sets of modern prints or striking black-and-white photographs. But traditional and contemporary styles can be juxtaposed to great effect. Furniture is an example: neutral slubbed or ribbed fabrics can be used to upholster an antique chair or club fender.

TraditionalDecorativeThemes

The idea of the library as a masculine domain can be accentuated by a Gothic scheme, the decorative style that dominated early nineteenth-century libraries with its connotations of antiquity and mediaevalism that conjured an atmosphere of historical learning. Such a mood was no doubt endorsed by volumes of Horace Walpole's Gothic novel

The Castle of Otranto (1764), and Walter Scott's *Waverley* novels (1814–31). The Gothic preponderence for dark wooden panelling, carved oak furniture and dominant fireplace have influenced traditional library decoration to the present day. The tangential influences of Jacobean and Elizabethan styles can contribute to the period effect.

Neo-classicism is an alternative style that ran parallel to the Gothic strain, where inspiration from Ancient Greece, Egypt and Rome became an expression of culture and civilization. Neo-classicism has an imposing, at times decayed splendour, characterized by the Regency architect Sir John Soane, whose schemes of coral pink, porphyry red, sienna yellow and ochre echo the colours of classical marble. The distinctive arched alcoves, doors and windows, the mirrors set strategically above fireplaces and doorways, on vaulted ceilings and beside windows to give an illusion of space and light – all these elements could inspire a contemporary room decorated on a less towering scale.

A Contemporary Look

An alternative is to create an airy colonial atmosphere in a pale understated scheme where neutral shades of stone, buff and ivory change with the interplay of light and shadow. As daylight is such an important element, this style is enhanced by a south-facing room with large windows or French doors leading onto a veranda or terrace. But without abundant natural light, cleverly placed mirrors – perhaps inspired by Soane's examples – and generous lighting can establish a calm, sunny ambience that makes an original backdrop to a collection of books or pictures.

As a degree of surprise is refreshing in a modern setting, the traditions of library style can be approached from a contemporary angle.

Books could become an unobtrusive element glimpsed behind a white wickerwork or wooden latticed frontage that dominates the wall space. A floor could be of bleached wooden boards or terracotta tiles for a Mediterranean effect. Low, streamlined sofas and armchairs exude comfort, covered in a quiet spectrum of calico and slubbed cottons.

A pale airy room flooded with natural light adds a contemporary twist to library tradition. This understated effect is achieved by the simplest scheme of white paintwork, white carpet and open shelves. A cultured touch comes from the Regency chair.

Creating the Style

Whatever style you choose to follow, the essentially calm atmosphere is established by a *laissez-faire* approach. It is a room with a settled air that emanates from leaving things as they are – which requires an indulgent attitude to the piles of books and papers ready for reference and browsing, stacked on a drum library table, capacious writing table or desk, or piled on the floor between comfortable armchairs.

In his *Encyclopedia of Taste and Architecture* (1833), J. C. Loudon advises that: 'A library should present a great contrast to the light elegance of the drawing-room with walls of a dark colour.' Today the library is no longer a male bastion, but rich deep colours still convey a traditional mood, toned with softer, lighter colours that keep the room from becoming too overpowering.

Colour and Pattern Decoration in a library should give an impression that the room has always existed. The colour scheme must provide a harmonious backdrop for the books and assorted studious elements and ornaments on view. The effect can be strong without being flamboyant; a bold pattern in a limited colour range gives unity and a sense of purpose to the room. Think of a palette drawn from Persian carpets, from paisley shawls, antique tapestries and deep tartans in a spectrum of crimson, dark green, navy or plum.

Pattern itself is a way to accentuate the studious air of a room decorated in a library style: classical motifs of acanthus leaves, symmetrical geometrics, Gothic trefoils and quatrefoils all instate an atmosphere of erudite tradition.

Such strong colours have an affinity together and can be combined without the oppressive effect that comes from too many primaries in one room. There are classic combinations to consider: navy, burgundy and tan, lightened with sand or cream; deep plum with shades of sage and cream; crimson with stone; jade with terracotta. With such strong tones, pure white can introduce too much of a stark contrast, so the lightening tones are best kept in an underplayed range of sand, stone or ivory. Paler schemes may suit a naturally dark room, or one where the library element is an accessory, rather than the focal point. Neutral combinations of buttermilk and sand, or grey and white have a light contemporary feel appropriate to a modern urban setting.

Deep tones of plum, burgundy and sage combine to create a rich, sophisticated interior, lightened by subtle shades of sand and taupe. The discreet sprigged pattern of the burgundy curtains is expanded on the piped cushion and border linking the two prints. A fine pin-striped wallpaper brings contemporary style to the room.

Texture This is an important decorative dimension that has special significance in a library setting, whether a traditional or contemporary scheme. Contrasting textures can be as interesting as combining colours or patterns, and often more appealing visually in a room already furnished with eye-catching books and diversions. Consider the contrast of matt upholstery fabrics against the sheen of glazed chintz cushions, of slubbed cotton or hessian with smooth felt or loden. Combining the classic library hallmarks of wooden panelling, leather, brass, parchment, tapestry and corduroy with finer textures of wickerwork, rattan, gilt, damask-weave cottons and chintz adds a femininity to the room that alleviates an overpowering sense of tradition.

Walls and Windows

With any room decoration it helps to have a starting point to guide ideas of colour and pattern. In a library, books are an element that give both structural and atmospheric suggestions. The presence of bookcases determines the style and extent of wall decoration, while the books themselves add an extra dimension of texture and colour.

Paint, Paper and Panelling If the walls are dominated by bookcases or shelving it is more effective to treat the remaining wall space as background. Choose a paint colour or com-

panion print wallpaper as a simple yet strong foil, reserving the master print for the curtains or upholstery. Panelling, an essential feature of the antiquarian style, could be conjured with *trompe-l'oeil* paintwork grained to resemble oak (either new and light or old and dark), beech or walnut – the classic library woods. Wallpaper can be distressed for a period effect by painting a coat of ageing varnish over the surface – a technique devised in the eighteenth century to preserve precious wallpaper, giving it a lacquered finish.

LEFT *A lighter look is achieved with delicate cane-seated chairs and strawberry cotton cushions which add a feminine softness to the substantial knee-hole desk.*

BELOW *Panelling can be created effectively with* trompe-l'oeil *paintwork and the use of deep paper borders.*

that might have lined a seventeeth-century closet? Linen union is a contemporary counterpart, transported back in time by tapestry prints or Elizabethan flamestitch.

Wall Hangings Carpeting, originally displayed on the table before descending to ground level, could also double as a wall hanging, reminiscent of Scotch carpet, a durable flat woven carpet that warmed closet walls in the eighteenth century. Richly coloured kelims or Turkish carpets suspended as wall hangings recall the oriental mood that Victorian men favoured for their studies and smoking rooms, conjuring the romantic mystery of the East. For the Scottish baronial look, a fashion set by Walter Scott at his house Abbotsford and later by Queen Victoria at Balmoral, use tartan as a wall covering, echoing the plaid on a matching sofa, or with a warm tartan rug tucked into a deep armchair.

ABOVE *An unquestionably masculine enclave, reserved for reading and relaxation in secluded comfort. Rich shades of burgundy, navy and tan steep the room in tradition while the robust stripes and paisleys furnish the air with oriental mystique. The Empire day bed has been given a grand treatment with a swagged, fringed wall hanging, draped nonchalantly over a wooden pole; its striped lining echoes the tailored bolster cushions and wallpaper.*

RIGHT *Matching curtains and walls gives bold impact to a scheme and presents a unified backdrop for subsidiary furnishings.*

Fabric for Walls Wallpapers drawn from textile sources enhance a period look. A small abstract or stipple pattern gives an illusion of a two-dimensional surface. Or for an authentic effect, why not apply the fabric itself to the walls, recalling both the texture and pattern

Windows Choose a treatment that is sympathetic to the scale and balance of the room. Where walls are a focal point, whether strongly patterned or book-lined, the curtains need to blend into the overall decoration without standing out as a separate feature. Where the walls are more of a backdrop, the curtains can come forward in a striking pattern or bold colour. Daylight is a crucial element of the study or library that should not be obscured by imposing curtains or pelmets, but curtains do need to be generously full to give that settled atmosphere of tradition.

Fabric for Windows The texture of curtain fabric is important. A linen union, slubbed dobby weave, loden or velvet all have a visible durability. A satin-weave cotton or chintz creates a lighter effect. As the glaze adds luminosity and movement to the fabric, chintz is a marvellous way to use rich, dark colours in

Oak panelling instates an almost tangible sense of the past; a powerful feature that becomes the starting point of any decoration. This room brings Georgian grandeur alive with a scheme of regal colour and texture that complements the panelling. The tapestried sofa with symmetrically paired cushions, a classical balance of furniture and magnificent Persian carpet all heighten a mood of stately splendour.

a library without the accompanying bulk of a velvet or thicker woven material. Alternatively, a pale glazed chintz acts as a restful foil to a cluttered room and a contrast to dark woodwork and leather bindings. It is a room where overt newness looks out of place. Fabrics need a patina of age that comes with subtle colouring, the nature of the pattern, or by physically distressing new materials in a bath of weak tea – or coffee for a stronger tone. A sand or cream background conveys an aged look more convincingly than a fresh white ground. For an underplayed effect, consider using the reverse side of a fabric. It gives a faded quality to the print.

Curtain Style The style of curtains and pelmets is obviously influenced by the shape and size of the windows. With a precedent for tradition in a library, treatment should be bold without being too full-blown. Tall sash windows suggest a Georgian festoon-tailed or deep pleated pelmet, edged in corresponding braid or bullion fringe. A striking and light-saving effect where there are two windows on a wall is to hang one curtain only at the far side of each window, linking the pair with a swagged pelmet that recalls an Empire scheme of 'continued drapery'.

Gothic windows can be accentuated by an arched lambrequin pelmet, the shape of which

RIGHT *A simple window seat provides a tranquil place to linger over a book or the view — propped up against a plump cushion that repeats the olive-green trim of the curtains.*

BELOW *Panelled shutters drawn across a wide window create a clean, uncluttered backdrop to a room filled with absorbing detail and strong colour. The narrow contours of the cream-painted woodwork harmonize with the geometric outlines of the bookcases, desk and knole sofa, and supply an effective foil for the arched Gothic screen.*

could reflect a crenellated or arched outline on the bookcases. Stained glass is a characteristic detail of Gothic windows that might be conjured by translucent oil paints over clear glass.

Blinds These are a useful solution to awkwardly shaped and positioned windows. A classic pleated roman blind has an appropriate dignity for a library living room, its straight edges enhanced, perhaps, by a tasselled fringe. Where curtains might be excessive or too light-absorbent, the elegant simplicity of a seventeenth-century window could be evoked with hinged wooden shutters. If a complete lack of curtain feels too spartan, soften the outlook with an understated swag looped over a wooden pole above the windows, or a more geometric hanging that reflects the contours of the shutters or bookcase. A rectangular window could be 'gothicized' by a blind painted with a *trompe-l'oeil* pointed arch.

Window-seats Any possibility of creating a window-seat in the bay of a deep sash or casement window should be taken up: a comfortable corner to sit and contemplate the garden or read a book suits the leisurely aspect of the room. The seat can be upholstered to match the curtains with an attached valance, given a Regency squab cushion, or piled with a nest of tapestry, velvet and chintz cushions. It could be the perfect niche to enjoy warmth from a boxed-in radiator below the window.

Bookcases

Bookcases give an architectural definition to the room in a traditional or contemporary style. Besides their practical use, they offer potential for decorative effects, borrowing ideas from past centuries. The open compartmental shelving of a seventeenth-century

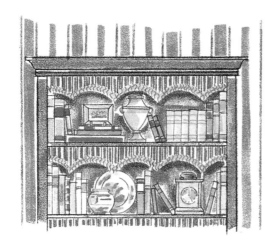

ABOVE LEFT *An elegant Regency-style bookcase continues a decorative theme with finely striped, scalloped fabric secured along each shelf.*

ABOVE RIGHT *A bookcase of architectural inspiration with broken pediment and carved mouldings serves a contemporary purpose, storing television and records besides books, pictures and a classical bust.*

BELOW LEFT *A classical glazed bookcase, which blends in with the wall decoration, is papered with a striking crimson interior.*

BELOW RIGHT *A Gothic bookcase with shelves glimpsed through latticed arches furnishes a mood of Victorian tradition.*

closet has an informality that might suit a small cosy study. Traditional leather-bound volumes have a reassuring dignity about them, while modern hardbacks in bright dustjackets or paperbacks introduce a pleasing variety of colour and pattern that undoes an over-decorated look. As well as books, the compartments are a perfect place to display china, keep glasses and drinks, a small television set or musical equipment and speakers.

Georgian-style bookcases are imposing, consuming an entire wall from floor to ceiling. Regency shapes are less substantial and lower in height, leaving space above for pictures, classical statues and busts. Inspiration can be drawn from these styles today, using wood grained to resemble oak or beech, or painted in a pale colour such as a muted jade green as a surprising contrast to the traditional contents. The bookcases and wall can be decorated in the same style and colour, with a trimming or border finishing off the shelves to give defin-ition to the bookcase. Alternatively, a contra-sting wallpaper or paint colour inside the shelves can provide a perfect foil for the books. Classical details can be introduced with pedimented shapes, or a row of carved urn or obelisk finials along the top of the shelves. Bookcases are a natural vehicle for Gothic decoration, with a castellated outline and shelves contained within pointed arches.

Open-plan bookcases painted in the same colour as the walls have a more contemporary appearance, especially where the shelves are unevenly spaced. The irregularity can be emphasized by storing an intentional mixture of books, ornaments, glass, flowers and trailing plants together. As an alternative to wood, shelving of clear or smoked glass adds a sense of space and reflected light to displays of *objets d'art*. For an added illusion of depth, the shelves could be backed with mirror glass.

Authentic details may be reinstalled for a period effect. Before bookcases were glazed, fringes were attached along the shelves to protect books from dust: an idea to copy today with bullion fringing, or a braid or gimp that picks out the key colours of the room. Or the idea of curtains hung inside a bookcase to shield against sunlight could make an original extension of the window treatment. Where visible, wall space behind the shelves needs consideration. It could be painted a stronger

Curtains hung inside a glazed bookcase protect precious bound volumes from strong sunlight. At night the opened doors become a decorative element, displaying the book bindings and adding related colour and fabric to the room.

colour to sharpen a recess effect; or lined with a companion print wallpaper, or perhaps a dark green or crimson felt for a club-like impression.

The most basic plywood shelving can be transformed with a covering of fabric. A striped cotton or geometric pattern that tones with the decorative scheme could be secured with brass tacks and pleated into a short valance suspended from each shelf.

Studious elements can be played up by an alphabetical index or literary motto scribed along the bookshelves. The antiquarian look of a diagonal wire grille across books can be imitated almost indistinguishably with chicken wire that has been blackened or sprayed gold and secured into open frames. Illusion is a cunning device in library decoration. A popular Victorian trick to conceal doors and cupboards was to make additional bookshelves from dummy book spines stuck straight onto the wall. The lower section of bookshelves makes a useful area to conceal radiators, or a television, video, records and tapes behind a decorative grille of wire mesh, wooden lattice, painted or natural wickerwork.

In a large, irregularly-shaped room, a recess for books could be established in a deep alcove or bay of a projecting window. The area can convey a secluded air of privacy, emphasized by a comfortable chair or cushioned banquette for sitting and browsing.

Furniture and Furnishings

Furniture While creating an atmosphere conducive to relaxation and entertaining, the furniture establishes an air of bookish comfort. It should be substantial without making the room appear over-furnished or cluttered. Today there is seldom the space to divide a room into areas for simultaneous reading, conversation, games or study. Instead the furniture arrangement can help to define the balance between study and relaxation.

Organization The fireplace is a natural focal point to work from when deciding on the right

LEFT *A classic scroll armed sofa of ample proportions is positioned appropriately beside the bookcase for easy browsing. The neutral linen upholstery is smartened with bold crimson piping and a heavy bullion fringe, echoed by the paisley shawl draped along the sofa back.*

ABOVE *A literary motto inscribed in fine calligraphy along the bookshelves plays up a cultured mood and stamps the room with a personal touch.*

arrangement for your furniture. A pair of sofas or armchairs could be positioned at right angles either side of the chimney piece, leaving space in front of the fire for a leather-topped club fender and a low spacious table to hold books, newspapers and magazines. An alternative to the twentieth-century coffee table could be a Victorian ottoman or low tapestried stool, a tôle or polished mahogany butler's tray on legs.

Furnishings The contours of furniture can be accentuated by a well-chosen print. The sweeping curves of a paisley upholstery fabric enhance a round-buttoned Tudor chair or chesterfield, while the angular lines of a knole sofa or wing armchair suit a geometric trellis, flamestitch or diamond weave in a plain fabric. In a low-ceilinged room, striped upholstery on upright armchairs lends an extra sense of height.

Cushions enhance the feeling of comfort as well as giving textural interest to the scheme. As a flexible and inexpensive element of decoration they are one of the simplest ways to make subtle variations to a living-room scheme, such as a seasonal switch of colour, texture or pattern.

To diffuse excessive tradition, introduce an element of the unexpected. A rattan maharajah's chair padded with paisley and chintz cushions, a painted Gothic throne, a *chaise-longue* or campaign chair on wheels bolstered with tartan rugs, all add character and a sense of humour to the room.

Tables and Desks Small tables at the end of a sofa or beside an armchair make an essential surface for reading lights or a collection — perhaps of paperweights or snuff boxes — that accentuates past traditions. An antique revolving bookcase could adapt into a useful side table, a forerunner to today's magazine rack originally found in a Victorian or Edwardian library for keeping books and periodicals within easy reach.

A large round table lacking antiquity or special beauty can be covered in a fringed loden cloth or table carpet. It can also conceal a television set or video when not in use, hidden behind a heavy floor-length cloth that draws apart on a curtain track, disguised by a deep fringe around the rim of the table.

The style and position of a desk is important:

ABOVE *There is no reason why a carpet should not be spread over a table instead of the floor. This Indian dhurrie brings a surprising dimension of colour and texture.*

RIGHT *An elegant eighteenth-century bureau deserves a prominent place in a room; a classic antique that blends happily into this mildly eccentric interpretation of Georgian-style decoration.*

Furniture Style A mix of classic styles and shapes recalls the deliberately disparate furnishings of an antiquarian style library. The same cross-period approach could continue by pairing an upholstered chesterfield sofa with an upright Georgian knole sofa. The collapsible arms of the knole sofa give it a surprising informality, perfect for lounging with a book beside the fire. Wing armchairs add traditional style but are impractical for conversation when placed side by side. Smaller semi-upholstered 'elbow' chairs are more versatile and light enough to move around the room.

whether it becomes an integral feature of the room or is tucked away in a recess or corner. Antique desks underline a traditional atmosphere, but as an outstanding piece of furniture they add style to a contemporary scheme. The classics are an elegant Georgian mahogany bureau with a sloping lid that folds down to a flat writing surface, a substantial Victorian roll-top desk with a galleried top and curved sliding front, or a pedestal desk on a plinth base with two columns of drawers. A rectangular Regency sofa table could be used as a writing desk, set in its classic position behind a sofa, parallel to the window. Or borrow a practical idea from the seventeenth-century library at Ham House of a vertical wooden flap that pulls down from the wall to form a flat writing desk. When not piled with books or papers, space could be found for decorative accessories like a marbled blotter, an antique desk set or photograph albums illuminated by a brass desk light. A round table set in the curve of a deep bay window might be an ideal place to work during the day. Or in a small informal room a recess

beside a projecting chimney-breast could provide a niche for a desk that does not encroach on the floor space. A pedestal desk or table could be installed with shelves for storage on the facing and side walls. Or a simple wooden work surface could be built in as a fixture, with room below to store filing cabinets, a typewriter and large waste-paper basket.

Floor and Fireplace

Floor The floor of a study library continues the mood of well-founded tradition. With an abundance of rich, deep tones, it needs to retain a neutral, unimposing quality. Pale floorboards can be waxed to a soft shine, or stained or grained for a period effect. Stencilling in a palette of brown on brown could conjure the decorative timber board patterns that were a feature of seventeenth-century interiors – or Gothic geometrics reminiscent of Pugin's characteristic design for the Houses of Parliament.

A deep wall-to-wall carpet in a neutral colour adds a gracious air of luxury and comfort.

FAR LEFT A small table with drawers for pens, pencils and paperwork doubles as a compact desk; portable enough to move into the light from an uncurtained window.

LEFT Space for study can be made at a table under the eaves of a sloping roof, where traditional desk accessories are neatly displayed against a starched linen cloth.

The marquetry effect of this wooden floor has a subtle three-dimensional quality, its closely related colours reflecting the tonal wallpaper pattern.

RIGHT *A classical column lamp adds a scholarly presence to the corner of a desk or table, paired with a pleated burgundy shade that reduces the light to a gentle glow.*

BELOW *The glowing colours of this Turkish carpet enclose the room with a sense of warmth and comfort. Its palette of navy, terracotta and moss green lay the foundation for a rich decorative scheme.*

Coconut or rush matting has a more understated academic look and provides a natural backdrop for a scattering of needlepoint rugs and faded Turkish carpets in mellow colours that offset the solidity of books or panelling. A thick underlay provides resilience. A respectable Victorian substitute for carpet was a floor covering of thick green baize, often smartened with a black border around the perimeter. The same effect could be created by a double thickness of woollen underlay: a baize green laid over a visible border of black.

Fireplace A fireplace is an important element, and its visual appeal is just as significant as its practical application; without it a room can lack a much-needed focal point. The illusion of a fireplace can be improvised with a wooden or marbled fire surround and mantelshelf framing a purpose-built recess in the wall. Imitation gas logs make a comfortable

glowing substitute for a real fire. Alternatively, a fireplace can be purely decorative, with a permanent *trompe-l'oeil* firescreen painted across the hearth.

A large existing fireplace can be played up with a traditional club fender, made wide enough to be a comfortable seat rather than a perch in front of the fire. The fender seat could be leather in true gentleman's club style, or upholstered in a textured linen union or weave that repeats the curtain or upholstery fabrics. Deep bullion fringing secured with brass tacks along the outer edge of the seat adds a bold flourish to the fireplace. A spacious marble, slate or tiled hearth makes a useful area for traditional fireside equipment: a toasting fork, tongs and poker resting on brass firedogs, ready to cook muffins and chestnuts for winter teas.

The mantelshelf provides a useful ledge for small pictures on stands, favourite art postcards and a Gothic or lantern clock. Alternatively it can serve as a testament to learning with a pair of classical figures or an obelisk at each end. An overmantel mirror brings a valuable source of light to the room – or the space can be dominated by a fine ancestral portrait or tapestry wall hanging.

Library upholstery extends to the seat of this fine brass fender, covered in a smart stippled cotton with a corresponding braid trim. Beside the poker, tongs and toasting fork there remains space for a dog basket, padded with a soft plum cushion.

Lighting

A library living room needs to be well lit, but never uniformly. Table lamps that brighten strategic areas with overlapping pools of light give the room a far more interesting atmosphere than the even effect of overhead illumination. Lamps based on classical shapes have an appropriate dignity, such as geometric wooden columns that echo the vertical spines of books or elegant silver stands adapted from tall Victorian candlesticks. An original swinging arm brass desk lamp with an adjustable shade, or an Argand oil lamp or wooden lantern could be discovered in a country antique shop or saleroom. A standard lamp saves space on a desk or table top and can be moved when necessary to cast light from behind a chair or table. A Victorian-style standard lamp with an adjustable brass stem and tripod base adds a period touch to the lighting scheme. Picture lights hung above paintings or bookshelves throw soft pools of light, adding interest to different corners of the room.

Lampshades These have a decorative and practical influence on the overall effect. Their colour, texture and proportion to the lamp base need considering. Opaque card or plain fabric shades in conical or 'coolie' styles have a classic simplicity, especially in pale neutral shades of cream and off-white where the light is diffused gently. Lining the shade with a pale pink fabric or paint adds a warm glow to the room.

Decorative Details

Besides books and pictures, library style needs a wealth of detail and accessories to establish an atmosphere that is studious, but never too solemn. Antique elements bring an air of culture and learning: a classical statue or marble bust, an old-fashioned globe or set of library steps all accentuate the feel of the room, while fitting into a contemporary context. Evidence of the games that were an essential feature of the eighteenth-century library can be incorporated today. Backgammon and chequerboards make decorative features on low tables or a flat needlepoint stool. Where space allows, a set of carpet bowls could provide a rainy-day diversion.

Pictures These are an essential area of library decoration, continuing its role as a showcase

for Grand Tour collections. Rich, deep colour schemes can be enhanced by dominant portraits, landscapes or still lifes, hung in important frames – combined with sets of prints, mezzotints and architectural drawings. Contemporary collections could be improvised by mounting sets of colourful stamps, maps or postcards in simple gilt frames and grouping them symmetrically on the walls. The contrast

of old versus modern can look striking: modern paintings against old leather volumes, or eighteenth-century arts and antiquities displayed against a backdrop of modern books. Where bookshelves occupy too much wall space, an important picture could be displayed on an easel in a corner of the room. Informality is accentuated by hanging a picture or two from the shelves in front of the books – a device similar to the seventeenth-century art of displaying a portrait over a tapestry. Wrapping a picture chain with a cover of taffeta or chintz adds a surprising softness and feminine detail to an essentially masculine room.

THE FAMILY ROOM

The family room is a living room in the literal sense: a focal point of the house, flat or cottage where the household might congregate to watch television, play games, sew or read; where children do their homework, where informal meals are eaten and friends entertained. It is a multi-functional space that accommodates a span of pursuits and ages.

The earliest family room was the Great Hall of a mediaeval manor house, a room where the entire household, from the noblest lord to the most humble serf, ate and caroused as one loyal family.

Throughout history to the present day, the hall has maintained a ceremonial, traditionally English role as the setting for banquets. On arrival at a great house, it was the hall that created a first impression, with its flagstoned or marble floor, gallery of family portraits and blazing log fire – a cavernous space often rising through two storeys with a sweeping central staircase to the first floor *piano nobile*. When the reception rooms moved downstairs in the eighteenth century, the hall became essential to the circuit of living rooms as an area for dancing that linked the dining and drawing rooms together.

The Victorians revived the idea of the hall as a living room, harking back to the Gothic image of the lord and master at home in his castle. In spite of its often impractical size and draughtiness, the hall became an unsegregated family room, where men could both smoke and keep female company. A raised minstrels' gallery at one end recalled mediaeval music-making, and a long refectory table served for celebratory dining occasions, watched over by suits of armour and trophies from sporting and military battlefields.

The Edwardians continued this trend noted by a house guest of the day as 'a strange Edwardian fashion of sitting not in one's sitting room, but in the hall outside it.' But these family rooms grew more comfortable than their Victorian precedents, filled with sofas, screens, a palm tree or two and a grand piano.

On a more accessible scale, inspiration can be drawn from the family room of a rural cottage where a crowded household lived, ate and often slept. Rustic decoration in the eighteenth and nineteenth centuries was determined more by basic necessity than visual concern. But where the cottager prospered, the family room evoked an atmosphere of tangible cosiness, as Flora Thompson describes in *Lark Rise to Candleford* (1945).

Walls and ceiling sponged in muted tones of straw and sage green create a mellow autumnal ambience in this spacious family room. A simple apple design stencilled above the dado rail gives a focus to the uncluttered walls and unites the L-shaped elements of the room, its path echoed by the painted dado rail and skirting below. The apple motif is repeated on the fruit-patterned chintz which makes a perfect companion to the gleaming country furniture.

In the Great Hall, a shortage of space was never a problem. But today the concept of a multi-purpose room often evolves from a confined living area, or the needs of modern life, where one family room has to encompass the assorted demands of adults, children, guests and animals.

Choosing a Style to Suit the Room

The relaxed atmosphere of a family room can be inspired by a rustic cottage or farmhouse

style if you have a room with irregular proportions, nooks and crannies or low beams. Alternatively, a tall airy space such as the top floor of a high-ceilinged Victorian building, flooded with light, can recall a more Bohemian studio atmosphere, accentuated by a bold use of colour and pattern. In a city, a light open space can be more inviting than two or three cramped rooms which, with a little imagination, can be turned into one large living room that serves as sitting, dining and sleeping areas.

A Rustic Family Room

This multi-purpose nature recalls the humble family room that formed the backbone of cottage life. Today's counterpart, whether in the town or country, has the practical advantages of warmth and comfort which were seldom inbuilt fixtures of the rustic tradition. But the relaxed quality of a living room inspired by cottage or farmhouse style is especially appropriate for a family with children, where a supply of toys and daily clutter preclude any air of sophistication. This homely room makes no pretence at concealing the various activities that take place.

Creating the Style

The decoration, furnishings and contents establish an air that is durable, without any obvious signs of being utilitarian. A sofa and armchairs may be on the shabby side, but they appear generous and inviting, with loose covers of faded floral chintz or quietly patterned linen union. Bare floorboards or rush matting are brightened with colourful rugs.

The room is warmed by an open fire and scented with fresh flowers and pot-pourri, while the reassuring tick of a grandfather clock adds stability to the family atmosphere. There is a strong personal quality, evoked by idiosyncratic collections of antique bric-à-brac and walls hung with photographs, children's paintings, framed samplers, watercolours or decorative china plates.

Walls and Windows

Paper and Paint Wall treatment depends on the size and proportions of a room. With uneven sloping or beamed walls, paint is the easiest cover to apply, while a quiet sprigged or stippled paper adds surface interest to smooth walls or can be used to hide any imperfections. Wallpaper borders applied over paint, or to correspond with papered walls, can bring a ceiling down to cottage scale. Wood is an integral feature of rustic decoration: walls could be given a simple panelled wainscot of wooden planks from floor to dado level, with paper or paintwork above. The planks could be waxed to reveal their natural grain, whitewashed or coloured in a range of ice-cream pastel tones for a colonial clapboard style.

Stencilling This traditional form of country decoration pioneered by the American settlers can be used to embellish walls and furniture. A design may be applied on or above skirting boards, as a wall frieze, or around door or window frames. It can also be used in a continuous pattern, resembling a seventeenth-century block-printed wallpaper. Depending on your technique, the effect can be sharp and bright, using strong colour over pale ground, or worn and faded with a misty pattern diffused over a closely related colour. Stencils can echo the design in a curtain, tablecloth, loose

covers or cushions. A rambling rose is a classic motif that does not rely on too much precision for its effect – or consider a rustic fruit print of apples, grapes or a fresh country posy. The appeal of stencilled pattern is its versatility and its fresh, freehand quality which embodies the homely spirit of the family living room.

Ceiling An important element of the room, the ceiling has potential for both decoration and storage. Traditional cottage ceilings have low beams and joists that can be painted white for an extra sense of height or blackened for a Tudor effect. The custom of painting beams with regional patterns could be continued using naive stencilled motifs – or follow the practice of preserving beams with a milky blue limewash. A soft pastel ceiling gives a subtle contrast to the walls, adding an extra dimension to the decoration of the room.

An unadorned window treatment lets plenty of daylight brighten the room and leaves space on the sill for potted geraniums. This single fall of crisp cotton gingham has a rustic simplicity, framed by a procession of stencilled apples that pick out the coral and green of the curtain and cushion on the rush-seated chair.

The diverse nature of a family room calls for hard wearing furniture that sets a mood of durable comfort. This informal interior encompasses a living and kitchen area, glimpsed through open rafters that divide the space. A sprigged paper supplies a quiet background for the array of pattern that fills the room.

Windows Natural light is an important element of the room, and windows play a practical role as much as a decorative one. Crisp cotton curtains in country floral prints, a classic gingham check or ticking stripe give an appropriate simplicity. A cottage garden print of climbing sweet peas or hollyhocks provides an urban substitute for wild country flowers creeping in at the window.

There is no reason for each window to be treated in the same way: a blind might be more practical and less light-obscuring at a small window – or consider the country practice of insulating a room with sturdy wooden shutters that fold back into the recess of a deep sill. A boxed wooden pelmet adds a rustic touch, especially stencilled with a design that repeats the curtain print. Alternatively, curtains could be hung from rings on a smooth wooden pole, painted to match the walls.

Furniture and Furnishings

Furniture In a family room furniture is fundamental, but always comfortable. Sofas and armchairs must be sturdy enough to withstand active children, dogs and cats, yet soft enough to sink into while watching television, reading or listening to music. There is no call for a matching suite of chairs or covers, providing there is some rapport between the shapes and colours. A classic chesterfield or scroll armed sofa and armchair have an appropriate informality, covered in a tonal stippled print. As a change from pattern, a grainy linen union or corded ottoman fabric give a durable textured surface to pile with patchwork and chintz cushions.

Furniture Style A simple country atmosphere is epitomized by a fireside rocker or ladder-backed, rush-seated or Windsor chair. A classic country heirloom is the Welsh dresser, passed down through generations to display the best china and ephemera of daily life. A large or expandable table is necessary to convivial family gatherings, with chairs per-

Country furniture has a reassuring timelessness that emanates from its substantial and uncontrived nature. While essentially practical this sturdy oak chest and comb-back chair bring a sense of old fashioned craftsmanship to the room.

manently set around. Where a table stands against the wall, a bench or stools can be stored beneath and pulled out to seat extra guests. A space below a side table might make a suitable niche for a dog basket, tucked away from underfoot or small children.

Furnishings A tartan travel rug or patchwork quilt adds colour and practical cover, tucked over the cushions or draped across the back of a sofa. Floor cushions supply extra seating for children, and an upholstered blanket box — matching the curtains or cushion fabrics — can be used as a low table or seating, and for storage.

A gingham squab cushion adds a touch of comfort and fresh colour to a traditional Windsor chair.

Floor and Fireplace

Floor The style of floor is determined by the age of the room and its foundations. A durable yet warm surface is important, especially where children play on the floor. Cork tiles or closely woven matting give a resilient surface. Waxed or painted floorboards could be stencilled with a diamond design to suggest old-fashioned tiles or marquetry patterns. Where a

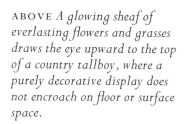

floor is overlaid with a large rug, a stencilled border can enhance the exposed boards.

With ingenuity, a variation of the floorcloth — the predecessor to linoleum that was popular in well-trodden halls and living rooms in the eighteenth and nineteenth centuries — could be reinstated. It was a varnished canvas mat, thickly painted with intricate geometric patterns or in imitation of oriental carpets, which could be redecorated when faded.

Fireplace The hearth, as the original source of warmth and light, is a traditional element of a family room. Wherever possible, an open fire gives character and a focal point to the room, but an allusion to the hearth can be suggested by a deep recess with a mantelshelf fixed above. The space could be given a tiled floor and contain an alternative heat source — perhaps a decorative *cuisinière* range or wood-burning stove — or it could house a television, video or music centre, become a book-lined recess, or a place to store children's toys.

Lighting

Lighting is a vital consideration in a multi-functional room. Where floor space is precious, wall brackets are a practical and safe alternative to table lamps. Providing a ceiling is not too low, a rustic metal chandelier or overhead pendant light with a wickerwork shade can look effective.

Decorative Details

The informal nature of a family room is accentuated by the profusion of both decorative and fundamental accessories that furnish walls and surfaces. The nooks and crannies that characterize country rooms – crammed with ornaments, crockery and plants – can be expanded into more ordered alcoves or large areas of shelving across the walls. These can be given decorative paintwork, with the shelves and interior walls stencilled, painted in a contrasting tone or a deeper shade of the master colour. Consider a terracotta alcove set into cottage pink walls, or rich butter yellow against a pale cowslip background. The contents can be part decorative, part practical, storing collections of china, glass, books and magazines dispersed among plants and vases of flowers.

An uncontrived composition of antique ornament and pictures gives a personal touch to a room. The randomly grouped, unframed oils on a geometric backdrop underline this informality, helped by the antique painted pine furniture, originally destined for attic bedrooms.

A Studio Scheme

A less disciplined approach is to treat a large living room as a studio, letting the room become a multi-functional space in which to work, relax and entertain. It is a scheme that works well in a tall top-storey room, filled with natural light from vast uncurtained windows and roof-top skylights – although with appropriate decoration, any large, well-lit room can create a studio atmosphere.

Creating the Style

The style has a Bohemian quality, accentuated by a bold use of colour and pattern, and an eclectic mix of artistic, family and functional furnishings. Working accessories help set the mood, while reflecting the professions and lifestyles of the occupants. The effect can be outwardly artistic with easels, print chests and walls crowded with paintings, or bear the spare, minimalist hallmarks of an architect, designer or photographer where natural light is the decorative key. The room could even conjure a dance studio with practice bar, wall mirrors and fabric screens.

Colour and Pattern As lofty open spaces tend to be cold and draughty, the interior needs to establish a feeling of warmth and comfort. Consider a palette of coral and grey or rose pink and jade green, both highlighted with white. The colours become a base for a striking mix of abstract pattern that adds a sense of rhythm and vitality and balances the proportions of a large room. Add depth to the scheme by spreading pattern across contrasting textures: mix fine voile and chintz against slub or ribbed cottons. However streamlined the decoration, let generous quantities of fabric introduce an air of comfort.

Walls and Windows

Paint and Paper A tall expanse of wall can carry off a striking decorative scheme that tempers the originality of the room's content. The scheme could combine both decorative paintwork and paper: *trompe-l'oeil* painting could suggest panelling from skirting to eye-level, below a wide striped or abstract floral wallpaper, creating an effect that is informal without appearing haphazard. Where an area is too massive to contemplate wallpaper, an original idea can be to block print a design over plain paintwork, perhaps picking out a motif from a furnishing fabric.

Windows As natural light is an essential ingredient of studio atmosphere, window decoration plays a minimal part in the scheme. A complete absence of curtains accentuates the outline of an arched or classic sash

window, while flooding the room with maximum light. If the effect is too stark, a simple roller blind can enclose the space at night and be drawn when needed by day to give shade or diffuse strong sunlight. Where windows remain unadorned, hang curtains across the corners of a room to soften the contours and form a practical cupboard or area of concealment where possessions can be stored out of sight.

LEFT *Unconventional curtains hung on rings from a twisted rope can be drawn across the corner of a room, forming an area of concealment or an impromptu hanging cupboard.*

BELOW *Lining the interior of these shelves with an abstract daisy wallpaper adds a bold touch of colour and pattern to practical storage.*

Tables and Screens Small tables draped with cotton cloths add colour and corresponding pattern, giving an essential lived-in feel to the area – especially when used to display flowers, fruit bowls, books and ornaments. Trimming the cloth with a contrasting cotton frill is an original alternative to a bullion fringe or tassels. Upholstered ottomans or painted trunks provide both storage and seating space and give an unconventional character to the furniture. Fabric-covered screens echoing the pattern in a tablecloth or cushion can be used at night to surround the entertaining space or to conceal a disordered work or play area from view.

Floor and Fireplace

Floorboards These can be stained and polished, varnished a mellow brown colour or painted white for a fresh, contemporary air and scattered with large, colourful rugs. Where the floor is needed to act as a calm foil to an exuberant scheme, look for a faded oriental carpet that complements the key colours, or perhaps a subtle-toned dhurrie.

ABOVE *A small table with its deeply fringed chintz cloth and cosy upholstered armchair instate a corner of tranquil comfort.*

RIGHT *An arched fabric screen covered in a pale grey and pink floral design interrupts the contours of a corner, while linking the bold wall and furnishing schemes together.*

Furniture and Furnishings

Amidst the 'working' environment a space devoted to relaxation is important, with sofas and low tables that adapt for an informal entertaining area as well as for sitting, dining and family activities. A pair of long sofas look more inviting in an open space than a group of armchairs. They can be upholstered in a linen union or printed cotton that relates to the walls, and piled with soft cushions of various shapes and textures – a mix of tapestry, crewel work, embroidery and plain cotton, trimmed with piping, fringes or tassels. Large floor cushions provide extra seating and an unusual ground level dimension.

Fireplace A fireplace in a studio adds a sense of homely comfort and provides a focal point to the seating area. Where non-existent, one could be suggested by a *trompe l'oeil* painting of a fire surround and mantelpiece, adding a three dimensional effect to the walls. But in an obviously modern setting, an imported fireplace could appear superfluous and distract from the open-plan studio atmosphere.

Lighting

The method of lighting needs to be determined by the scale, proportion and role of the room. In a tall-ceilinged space it is best approached on two levels, combining spotlights secured on tracks from the ceiling with free-standing angle poise reading lamps and large ceramic lamp bases with toning shades placed on the floor or low tables.

Decorative Details

A bold approach to pictures accentuates a studio atmosphere. Large walls need large pictures: contemporary oils, lithographs or prints that can be left unframed for an informal effect. The room feels more welcoming if pictures are hung at eye level and arranged in groups, especially in the seating area. Horizontal, rather than vertical hanging lowers large-scale proportions.

A sense of order and discipline maintains the balance of this urban-style living room. Pattern is limited to the vibrant fabric which covers the sofa and an abstract rug. A cool palette of grey, white and lemon yellow dominates, letting linear furniture take centre stage.

A balcony floor can be installed in an open light-filled room, creating a secluded place for sleeping, dining or playing. The airy galleried effect shown here makes practical use of all available space. The whole area is given simple cream paintwork which creates an uncluttered contemporary atmosphere.

An Urban Scheme

In the city, one light open space can be more inviting than two or three small rooms. A flexible and imaginative approach could incorporate a sitting, dining, sleeping and kitchen area into one spacious living room. The different elements can be played up or down to suit the scale and mood of the room — and, above all, your lifestyle. This open-space approach is informal, but it is a family room where the occupants need to maintain a sense of order. The key is to establish a neutral decorative scheme that unites the diverse functions of the room, without imposing too strong a message of period style, colour or

pattern. A sense of unity throughout is important and avoids divisions that decrease a feeling of space.

Creating the Style

The areas in a multi-purpose setting do, however, need a certain definition that can be achieved with subtle effects, both structural and decorative.

Defining Space A raised area or platform at one end of the room could mark out an area for eating or family activities. In a high-ceilinged room or studio, a balcony floor could be installed at one end, creating a sleeping area or unexpected dining floor away from immediate view. An open or spiral staircase is the most space-efficient and least light-absorbent method of access.

The art of concealment is important in a family living room where the emphasis is on sitting, entertaining and eating. Screens are a decorative and flexible feature that can be incorporated into a scheme, changing the balance of a room to suit the occasion; perhaps marking a division between seating and dining areas, or concealing a kitchen corner or children's play space from view. Besides excluding draughts in a large room, fabric-covered screens accentuate a decorative theme, echoing the print and colour of the upholstery or curtains. The outline, whether rounded, with Gothic arches or in a classical serpentine curve, could reflect the contours of pelmets, alcoves or shelving.

A more luxuriant effect is to create a fabric partition that draws like a curtain across the room at night enclosing a dining, or perhaps sleeping, space away from the main seating area. A romantic fall of printed voile, muslin or glazed chintz will give a fluid tent-like drape to be drawn after dinner, concealing the finished meal.

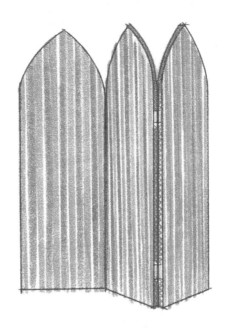

The Gothic arched outline of this screen is enhanced by bold Regency stripes.

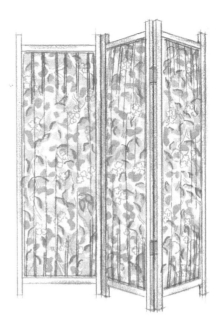

This wooden screen with softly pleated chintz curtains is appropriate for screening a sleeping area.

A classical serpentine screen, upholstered in a damask-patterned weave, forms an elegant backdrop to a candlelit dinner table.

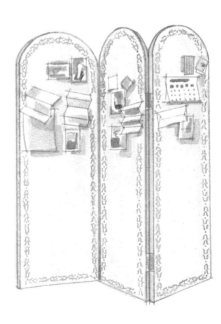

A simple arched screen, covered in colourful felt or green baize, makes an expansive pinboard for cards, calendars and notices.

ABOVE *This underplayed window treatment is accentuated by continuing the wallpaper onto the sill and recess of a deep set window. A plain roman blind maintains a linear simplicity, reflecting the quiet stripes and soft colour of the scheme.*

Walls and Windows

Paint and Paper Colours in a multi-functional room are best kept to a fresh gentle palette of one or two related tones. Accents of stronger colours can be introduced on loose covers, curtains, cushions or screens. Wallpaper or paint provides a uniform backdrop for pictures and wall furniture. Subtle tones of ivory, stone, taupe or light sunny shades of straw yellow, aquamarine or buttermilk emphasize an uncluttered open space. Understated stripes add height to a low-ceilinged room, while an abstract stippled paper gives a textured tonal effect without obvious pattern. Wallpaper ages less noticeably if it is of good quality and will withstand occasional cleaning. Paintwork needs to be immaculately applied for long lasting wear – perhaps a vinyl matt emulsion that contrasts with white satin gloss on the doors and skirting.

Storage If floor space is precious, the walls become a functional, as well as decorative, area: a space for fitted cupboards, bookshelves, alcoves, and wall units, where the demands of visual display and practical storage work together. If walls are deep enough, set-in recesses or alcoves provide storage space without intruding into the room. Alcoves, especially in a pair, can make an elegant feature, shaped in Palladian arches with well-spaced shelves to hold books, china, ornaments, a small television, radio or music centre. The interior of an alcove could be painted or papered in a variation of the room's master colour or print, or lined with fabric that matches the furnishings. The shelves could also be covered on both sides with a matt vinyl wallpaper, and a rectangular recess framed with a narrow wallpaper border or an outline of braid or gimp that tones with the wall colour.

An alcove or recess containing objects more functional than decorative can be treated as a cupboard, with its contents screened by a curtain. It could be a simple drape gathered and secured along the top of the recess, or take the form of a reefed curtain. The effect can be elaborated with a pediment style of pelmet made with a swathe of fabric and suspended over three projecting brackets.

Purpose-built wooden cupboards or wall units that look too new can be aged with a dusty blue colour wash to recall the bleached uneven patina of old Swedish pine. This is contrived by a thinned coat of smoke-blue emulsion which is wiped away while still damp, then followed by a deeper Prussian blue, rubbed with a cloth into protruding knots and surfaces to give two levels of colour.

Windows Continue the same underplayed mood as for the walls, adding a toning pattern to plain paint, or using a plain chintz or thicker textured weave against a patterned wallpaper. Alternatively, the windows can become a focal point of colour and decoration, with a bold floral or chinoiserie print that adds an air of country-house comfort to a contemporary scheme. The curtains need a restrained elegance, perhaps hanging from plain wooden or brass rods, without any pelmet or elaborate trimmings to let maximum daylight into the room. Sill-length curtains may be more practical, leaving space below for a window-seat, desk or table. Roman blinds or hinged wooden shutters have a timeless simplicity that accentuates a calm, ordered atmosphere.

Furniture and Furnishings

With a family room, practical considerations will affect your choice of colour scheme and fabrics for furnishings. But fundamental needs do not have to overrule a decorative style. With forethought both elements can combine successfully – and in this room a well-organized framework is essential.

Furniture A degree of improvisation can answer the diverse demands of a multi-purpose room. A comfortable divan can double as a sofa and spare bed, positioned alongside a wall and covered with a bank of soft cushions. A bolster at each end, suggesting a Regency couch, will give it a tailored, daytime look.

Without seeming utilitarian, fitted furniture becomes an integral part of the scheme. Cushioned bench seating against a wall, or built into the curve of a bay window, saves floor space from free-standing chairs. Space beneath the benches, hidden by a pleated valance matching the curtains or loose covers, can conceal cupboards for children's toys, clothes, bedlinen, china or glass.

A table standing in the window can be extended for dining, using the fixed bench or folding canvas chairs or stools for seats. A dining table need not stand permanently in position, but can be stored against the wall – a practice that continued into the eighteenth century before the dining room became an independent part of the house. An impromptu table can be made from a pair of occasional tables, heightened with bricks or heavy books and covered with a floor-length cloth. Its dimensions can change to match the occasion.

Furnishings It makes more sense to choose loose covers for easy cleaning rather than upholstery on sofas and armchairs; a diamond or slub weave, or a patterned upholstery fabric, is durable without appearing too obviously practical. A switch of cover, changing a plain colour for a pattern, or deep smoke blue for a pale summery apricot or ivory, can change the whole mood of the room in a subtle yet simple way.

A stylish Empire daybed set against the wall can double as a sofa, banked with cushions and textured rugs. The incongruous blend of Georgian armchair and modern leather recliner adds an eclectic originality to the room.

An absence of large pieces of furniture instates an airy open feeling, essential to a room where floor space is a valuable commodity. Ample cushions supply a versatile form of seating, well placed for the view from a floor level window.

Floor and Fireplace

Floor For an unobtrusive background that pulls the room together, try a fitted cord carpet or resilient jute matting which has a neutral and practical quality – preferably in a colour pale enough to add light to the room, yet dark enough to hide everyday wear and tear. For a bolder effect, a large dhurrie or kelim – fixed to stop it rucking – can add character and muted colour to the scheme. The floor of a kitchen corner could be tiled in the same tone as the base carpet or matting.

Fireplace A fireplace creates a bold focal point in a room and supplies a framework for decorative and practical ornament, while a fire surround of marble, polished wood or graphic tiles adds surface texture to a scheme. When not in use, the hearth could contain a modern sculpture or striking ceramic vase.

Lighting

Lighting is an essential feature that needs to be unobtrusive, yet appropriately sited to brighten specific corners of the room. Spotlights fixed from the ceiling or as high wall brackets could be backed up by a globe floor lamp or metal angle poise light for reading, accentuating the contemporary feel of the room. Modern ceramic vases, converted into table lamps, will also give the right look.

Decorative Details

In any functional room it is important to introduce elements of pure decoration that divert the eye. A collection of beautiful jugs, a striking modern sculpture, a set of prints or paintings add a distinctive hallmark of individual style. Even an extravagant fruit bowl has effective impact.

Flowers always add a touch of freshness to a room and can be used to highlight its principal colours. Displayed in groups of a single colour, they create a strong, contemporary statement, as does a single bloom in a sculptural vase. Natural forms, such as driftwood or geological stones, lend a subtle combination of colour and texture to a fireplace or tabletop and add character to a decorative scheme.

FAR LEFT *An elegantly carved marble fireplace cultivates tradition within a contemporary setting. The result is a subtle balance between past and present inspiration, combining classical sculpture with a stark arrangement of gnarled branches in the hearth.*

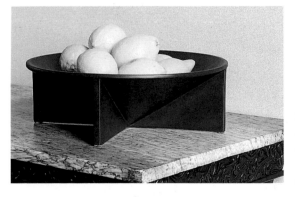

ABOVE *A discreet matt black lamp can be angled to cast shafts of light against a wall, illuminating selected* objets d'art *in the room.*

LEFT *Striking decoration need not be elaborate or expensive. A nest of lemons creates a brilliant splash of colour, framed by a black wooden bowl on a smooth marble backdrop.*

THE GARDEN ROOM

The very nature of a garden room, with its abundance of plants and glass, creates an informal, airy environment ideal for entertaining, quiet relaxation or reading. It may seem a luxurious concept, but once established, a garden room or conservatory soon becomes an integral part of the house – adding a sense of space and light to the adjoining rooms and enhancing the outdoor surroundings. Even on a dull, rainy day, the outlook appears more inviting viewed through an expanse of colourful plants and greenery. Whether a garden room can be used in winter as well as summer depends on the structure, glazing and setting, although unheated and single glazed, it still provides a place to enjoy winter sunshine.

The earliest garden rooms were built in the seventeenth century as orangeries to protect exotic fruit trees. A garden room as somewhere to spend time arose in the eighteenth century, when the Picturesque concept of architecture flourished.

A conservatory, which linked the drawing room to the garden, provided a perfect bridge with nature, as well as a romantic setting for plants, fruit trees and flowers. At first conservatories were an addition only for the landed gentry who had an income, country mansion and ranks of gardeners to match the scale of wooden and glass buildings pioneered by the landscape gardener and architect Humphry Repton. But the progress and affluence that came with the Industrial Revolution brought the conservatory, or the larger 'winter garden', well within reach of prosperous Victorians.

In the suburbs a modest garden room filled with foliage and flowers became a retreat from the industrialization that engulfed the landscape. In the newly acquired country seat, however, extravagant cast-iron and glass structures were erected, inspired by Joseph Paxton's conservatories at Chatsworth and Crystal Palace.

The conservatory fulfilled strong Victorian preoccupations, bringing elements of the natural world inside all year round. As well as size, its contents became something of a status symbol. Rare plants transported home from adventurous forays abroad were nurtured in the conservatory's temperate climate for display inside the house, often kept within a miniature greenhouse or wardian case, safe from the oil and gas fumes in the air. The conservatory also provided a comfortable, well lit setting for family photographs and the important ritual of Sunday afternoon tea.

Choosing a Style to Suit the Room

A south-facing setting is the ideal location for a garden room – preferably a light-filled area opening onto a sheltered terrace, which becomes an extension of the room in summer. Or it can be a custom-built glass conservatory adding extra light and space to a ground-floor apartment, house or cottage. In town, where a garden is often no more than a back yard, a conservatory filled with plants provides a more than adequate alternative to a real country garden, while expanding the scale and altering the whole mood of the house.

But scope for a garden style of room can also be found within the existing layout of a house. A light annexe or recess in a drawing room, decorated in keeping with the overall scheme, can take on the mood of a sun-filled garden room if given a few unmistakable *al fresco* touches. A profusion of plants and flowers adds a garden atmosphere to any room especially if complemented by a fresh palette of white, yellow and green. Pattern can intensify the garden effect – use a trellis wallpaper as a backdrop to plants, or a bold floral print to frame the view from large sash or French windows. Any natural wood can be emphasized by a tiled terracotta or bright Italianate chequerboard floor; alternatively a stone floor could be overlaid with rush matting. The garden room does not have to be part of the house at all. A pavilion, gazebo or summerhouse in a rambling garden has a natural seclusion that suits the romantic nature of this type of room. Nor need a garden room be confined to ground level. A balcony leading from the living room or bedroom of a town

FAR LEFT ABOVE *This nineteenth-century painting shows how a garden atmosphere can be conjured indoors and expresses the delights of a room filled with greenery and flowers.*

FAR LEFT BELOW *A south-facing setting is the ideal location for a garden room. A recess in a drawing room, decorated in keeping with the overall scheme, can take on the mood of a sun-filled garden with a profusion of plants.*

LEFT *The classic Victorian conservatory, with its tropical jungle of exotic plants and ferns complete with pendant chandelier.*

flat, shaded and sheltered from rain by a decorative awning, could be transformed into a small leafy garden room. Or you could create a roof terrace, furnished with rustic pots and comfortable garden chairs, creating a secluded oasis of greenery and cultivation amidst an urban skyline.

Creating the Style

Decoration in a garden room depends very much on how it is to be used. Is it to be an outdoor continuation of the interior, or a covered section of the garden? Where the room is needed as an extra living space,

A roof terrace is given a modern streamlined look to match its structure with regimental pots of trimmed evergreens.

domestic considerations such as heating and comfort are just as important as glass, greenery and sunlight. Decorative style is often prompted by the actual structure and position of the garden room: a streamlined contemporary design will obviously need to be treated very differently from a period piece of Gothic curved glass and cast iron. Whatever the style, it should be related to the period and mood of the house.

A Victorian Conservatory

The classic Victorian conservatory, with its tropical jungle of exotic plants, ferns and succulents, its wall mirrors and statues – or, on a more ambitious scale, its fountains and fishponds – provides endless inspiration for garden rooms today. These luxurious features provide the perfect backdrop for white or dark green wrought-iron furniture, bird cages, brass jardinières full of scented parma violets and wire hanging baskets trailing geraniums, fuchsias and lobelias.

An Edwardian-style Veranda

If the Victorian style does not suit, try a colonial Edwardian veranda with echoes of the Raj. White trellised walls, split cane blinds, a ceiling fan, rattan planters' chairs and tall potted palms on a marble floor create an oasis of light uncluttered calm.

A Mediterranean Garden Room

A typical Mediterranean garden room should have an abundance of colour and an evocative scent. The terracotta floors might be dotted with Italianate statues and comfortable wicker chairs padded with Provençal cotton cushions; the walls covered with jasmine, bougainvillaea and plumbago; and the air heavy with the pungent aroma of herbs – basil, wild thyme, rosemary, lemon and bay trees.

Colour and Pattern

In a room dominated by plants, the decoration becomes a backdrop that enhances the impression of sunlight and warmth. Pale neutral tones supply a gentle foil to brilliant flowers and foliage. Shades of cream, stone, pale taupe, sand, sage and apricot echo nature without competing for attention. Prints might have a fresh simplicity evoked by naive rustic sprigs or freehand florals in a restrained palette of green, white and terracotta. Or they might be more boldly designed with country roses, lilies, tulips or hollyhocks heightening a glorious profusion of real flowers and foliage. Fruit can be highlighted by a design that matches a particular colour or species.

A Mediterranean haven created with wicker furniture, trellis work on the walls and warm terracotta floor tiles.

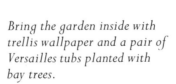

Bring the garden inside with trellis wallpaper and a pair of Versailles tubs planted with bay trees.

A window-seat becomes a floral arbour, its sills filled with decorative pots of spring bulbs.

Walls and Windows

Walls The treatment of walls depends on the structure and position of the room. Where a definite garden emphasis is required, bare stone or brick walls beneath a pattern of climbing plants will stress an *al fresco* mood. If more light is needed, the unplastered walls could be whitewashed, although a very pale brick pink or sage green might be more restful on the eyes since pure white can be uncomfortably dazzling in direct sunlight.

Special Effects A smooth plastered wall could be given texture by a wooden or bamboo trellis

cut into decorative arches and panels or used to support climbing plants. A green trellis will merge into foliage, but a white trellis on a terracotta painted wall has an Etruscan feel that can be played up with neo-classical statues and urns. In an indoor garden room, wall murals depicting an Arcadian landscape could be painted as a *trompe-l'oeil* view, recalling the picturesque style of the late eighteenth century.

Staging Plants As climbing plants do not guarantee permanent cover, walls can be furnished with tiers of pots arrayed on glass or wooden shelves. As different plants reach full bloom, the pots can be moved to the most prominent position on the shelves, thus ensuring a variety of scent and colour in the room throughout the year. The containers themselves can be as decorative as the plants: an assortment of flower pots, rush or wicker baskets, *cache pots* and old china bowls planted with spring bulbs.

Windows A glass structure can become unbearably hot in summer – and arctic in winter. Double glazing and central heating make a

A tented effect can be created with roof curtains of fine cotton voile, hung from rings on poles fixed to the glazing bars.

room habitable all year round (although there has to be a compromise between the needs of plants and humans), but protection from direct sunlight is essential with blinds that can be drawn across the roof and walls against the midday sun.

Blinds These can be of slatted cane or cedar that cast striped shadows across the room, or of pale cotton or sailcloth to diffuse the sunlight. Pleated roman blinds in a simple ticking stripe, or a stippled or sprigged floral print, have a fresh yet unobtrusive quality, introducing a pattern that can be echoed on cushions, tablecloth and napkins. In hot climates wooden blinds that roll down outside the glass absorb the heat before it penetrates the roof, diluting the force of the sun. Venetian blinds suspended from the roof interior introduce a contemporary graphic effect, casting striped shadows across the room. In less tropical conditions a tented effect can be created with roof curtains of fine cotton or voile hung from rings onto poles fixed to the glazing bars.

An alternative to fabric is to train a vine across the slope of a roof providing a canopy of shade and edible decoration. The evergreen backdrop can be entwined with a seasonal variety of passion flower, clematis or stephanotis.

ABOVE *Wicker chairs need generous padding with soft cushions.*

FAR RIGHT *A table large enough for impromptu meals is covered with a pretty floor-length cloth in a fresh botanical print.*

Furniture and Furnishings

Furniture An abundance of plants can create a crowded atmosphere. To offset this, furniture should appear light and delicate, with no impression of cluttering the room. This is the place for classic garden furniture that conveys an airy, informal mood. A mix of Lloyd Loom wicker chairs, Edwardian basket loungers, seats of bamboo, rattan and cane all evoke a summery feel, even in midwinter. Comfort is essential for lingering over meals or spending lazy afternoons curled up with a good book. Perhaps a well-secured canvas hammock could be strung across a corner of the room.

Furnishings Chairs need generous padding from soft cushions and bolsters of patchwork or frilled cotton covers. A table large enough for impromptu meals or an elegant candlelit dinner party is an important element of garden room furniture. It can stay permanently covered with a pretty floor-length cloth of cotton or lace that makes an attractive backdrop for bowls of fruit, flowers and scented plants. A china tea service painted with botanical designs can accentuate the colour and natural aspect of the room. Corresponding table napkins and squab cushions secured to upright chairs with decorative ties add finishing touches.

Floors

Tiles and Floorboards The floor plays an important part in creating the natural mood of a garden room. An outdoor setting is accentuated by terracotta or clay tiles or flagstones that can be watered as liberally as the plants. A mosaic or marbled chequerboard of black-and-white tiles could be laid for a striking Victorian effect. In an interior setting, rush matting overlaid with rag rugs or faded kelims gives a warm sunny feel to the room. Floorboards glossed in ivory or cream paint could be stencilled with trailing leaves to mirror an overhead vine or climbing plant, or perhaps painted with a *trompe-l'oeil* trellis or floral design.

Floor Plan This is affected by the method of indoor gardening. Plants can be grown from beds dug out from the floor, in raised beds along one edge of the room, or just in pots and

FAR LEFT *Pools of candlelight create a romantic backdrop to a summer dinner table.*

LEFT *A marbled chequerboard of black and white tiles creates a striking Victorian effect in this conservatory.*

Plants

However idyllic the surroundings, it is the plants themselves that furnish the room and convey its luxuriant atmosphere. Bare walls cry out for rapid covering by fast growing plants, many of which do well in the warm and sheltered conditions of a conservatory or garden room. *Cobaea*, a passion flower with bell-like violet or cream flowers, or *Eccremocarpus*, with its vibrant orange flowers, will climb walls long before slower-growing plants like scented jasmine, everlasting sweet pea, honeysuckle or the delicate butter-yellow rose *Banksia lutea* have time to spread themselves.

Above all, plants should bring a feeling of perpetual joy to the garden room. This is especially important in midwinter when there are no cut flowers from the garden to enjoy. We all know what a treat it is to have moss-lined bowls of narcissi and hyacinths around the house in winter months, but imagine the exotic delights of scented mimosa, rhododendrons and camellias in early January.

LEFT *Faded kelims over a warm terracotta tiled floor are combined with natural cane furniture for a Mediterranean look.*

controlled to a great extent by the lighting. Candles cast a gentle flattering glow over a dinner party, burning in elegant candelabras or more informally on antique china saucers entwined with flowers and foliage. A back-up of candlelight, flickering in glass shades or lanterns, can be interspersed with the plants on shelves at different levels around the room. Tall slow-burning candles rooted in urns and terracotta pots can give the impression of growing amongst the greenery, as well as lending an exotic sheen to the plants.

Electricity is a less time-consuming alternative, with dimmed spotlights angled from the glazing bars across the roof or directed upwards from ground level illuminating the walls and corners of the room. Spotlights shining from an outside border throw diffused light into the room. They could be raised on sticks if the light is obstructed by dense foliage. Statues, ponds or fountains can all be highlighted for a theatrical effect, and in a traditional conservatory an elegant period atmosphere may be recreated by the interplay of reflected glass from a chandelier overhead.

Decorative Details

In midsummer, a large cotton parasol fixed above the table provides extra shade at meal times. Add different levels of interest to the room with free-standing plant containers or decorative statues. Consider a pair of urns set on pedestals, planted with lilies or silver-leaved senecio and pansies, or a stone trough over-flowing with Mediterranean daisies and herbs. New stonework can be aged rapidly with a layer of soured milk that encourages moss and surface lichen to grow. Where space allows, water introduces a peaceful and re-freshing quality to the garden room, either as a gently splashing fountain or a calm fishpond floating with waterlilies.

ABOVE *A balcony provides a leafy retreat in which to have breakfast, surrounded by luxurious foliage.*

RIGHT *A large cotton parasol, fixed above the table, provides decorative shade in this beautiful nineteenth-century orangery.*

tubs staged around the walls and floor. Each scheme has its advantages. Once established in permanent beds, plants grow more vigorously across the walls and demand less attention, but a potted garden is more versatile and plants should thrive provided they are well fed and watered. Tubs can be rotated easily and winter flowering shrubs moved outside in summer.

Lighting

During the summer months a garden room can be used in the evening as well as during the day. It makes a perfect setting for entertaining, with aromatic tobacco plants, pungent herbs, night-scented stocks and jasmine conjuring a romantic Mediterranean atmosphere.

Nightlight At night the mood of the room is

LAURA ASHLEY SHOPS

Home Furnishing shops in the United Kingdom, Europe, United States and the Pacific Basin.

AUSTRALIA

The Gallerie,
Gawler Place,
ADELAIDE,
South Australia, 5000

1036 High Street,
ARMADALE,
Victoria, 3134

The Myer Centre,
Queen Street,
BRISBANE,
Queensland, 4000

Shop 84,
Wintergarden,
171 Queen Street,
BRISBANE,
Queensland, 4000

781 Burke Road,
CAMBERWELL,
Victoria, 3124

Shop 58,
The Gallery,
Lemon Grove,
Victoria Avenue,
CHATSWOOD,
N.S.W., 2067

Shop 353–355,
Harbourside Festival
Marketplace,
DARLING HARBOUR,
N.S.W., 2009

3 Transvaal Avenue,
DOUBLE BAY,
N.S.W., 2028

Shop 49,
Market Square,
Moorabool Street,
GEELONG,
Victoria, 3220

Centrepoint,
209 Murray Street,
HOBART,
Tasmania, 7000

Shop 12, Level 1,
Macquarie Centre,
NORTH RYDE,
N.S.W., 2113

179 Collins Street,
MELBOURNE,
Victoria, 3000

City Arcade,
Hay Street Level,
PERTH,
Western Australia, 6000

236 Swan Street,
(Balls Corner),
RICHMOND,
Victoria, 3121

Middle Level,
Nepean Hwy,
SOUTHLAND,
Victoria, 3192

462 City Road,
SOUTH MELBOURNE,
Victoria, 3205
(Decorator Collection)

Jam Factory,
Chapel Street,
SOUTH YARRA,
Victoria, 3141

Mezzanine Level,
Centrepoint,
Castlereagh Street,
SYDNEY,
N.S.W., 2000

114 Castlereagh Street,
SYDNEY,
N.S.W., 2000

AUSTRIA

Judengasse 11,
5020 SALZBURG

Weihburggasse 5,
1010 VIENNA

BELGIUM

Frankrijklei 27,
2000 ANTWERP

32 rue de Namur,
1000 BRUSSELS

81–83 rue de Naumur,
1000 BRUSSELS

Volderstraat 15,
9000 GHENT

CANADA

Sherway Gardens,

25 The West Mall,
Suite J6
ETOBICOKE,
Ontario M9C 1B8

2110 Crescent Street,
MONTREAL,
Quebec H3G 2B8

136 Bank Street,
OTTOWA,
Ontario K1P 5N8

2452 Blvd. Wilfrid Laurier,
STE. FOY,
Quebec G1V 2L1

18 Hazelton Avenue,
TORONTO,
Ontario M5R 2E2

1171 Robson Street,
VANCOUVER,
British Columbia V6E 1B5

2901 Bayview Avenue,
Bayview Village
Shopping Ctr,
WILLOWDALE,
Ontario M2K 1E6

Portage Place,
WINNIPEG,
Manitoba

FRANCE

4 rue Joseph Cabassol,
13100 AIX EN PROVENCE

2 place du Palais,
33000 BORDEAUX

18–20 rue Piron,
21000 DIJON

25 rue de la Grande Chaussée,
59800 LILLE

98 rue Président Edouard
Herriot,
69002 LYON

4 rue des Dominicains,
5400 NANCY

16 rue Crébillon,
4400 NANTES

Galeries Lafayette,
6 avenue Jean Médecin,
06000 NICE

94 rue de Rennes,
75006 PARIS

Galeries Lafayette,
40 bld Haussmann,
75009 PARIS

Au Printemps,
64 bld Haussmann,
75009 PARIS

Au Printemps,
Centre Commercial
Vélizy 2,
Avenue de l'Europe,
Vélizy Villacoublay,
78140 PARIS

Au Printemps,
Centre Commercial Parly 2,
Avenue Charles de Gaulle,
Le Chesnay,
78150 PARIS

19 rue du Gros Horloge,
7600 ROUEN

2 rue du Temple Neuf,
67000 STRASBOURG

Au Printemps,
Centre Commercial
'Grand Var',
Ave. de l'Université,
83160 La Valette,
TOULON

50 rue Boulbonne,
31000 TOULOUSE

HOLLAND

Leidestraat 7,
1017 NS AMSTERDAM

Bakkerstraat 17,
6811 EG ARNHEM

Demer 24a,
5611 AS EINDHOVEN

Hoogstraat,
32/Paleispromenade,
2513 AS
'S-GRAVENHAGE

M. Brugstraat 8,
6211 ET MAASTRICHT

Lijnbaan 63,
3012 EL ROTTERDAM

Oudegracht 141,
3511 AJ UTRECHT

IRELAND

60–61 Grafton Street,
DUBLIN

ITALY

4 Via Brera,
20121 MILAN

JAPAN

8–32,
Hondori,
Naka-ku,
HIROSHIMA

26–1,
Ekimae Honmachi,
Kawasaki-ku,
KAWASAKI

2–4–14,
Honcho,
Kichijoji,
MUSASHINO-SHI

3–14–15,
Sakae,
NAGOYA-SHI

6–10–12,
Ginza,
Chuo-ku,
TOKYO

1–26–18,
Jiyugaoka,
Meguro-ku,
TOKYO

3–8–15,
Akasaka,
Minato-ku,
TOKYO

MITSUKOSHI
IN-SHOPS:

1–7–1–119,
Achi,
Kurashiki-shi

1–4–1,
Muromachi,
Chuo-ku,
TOKYO

3–29–1,
Shinjuku,
Shinjuku-ku,
TOKYO

1–2–7,
Kitasaiwai,
Nishi-ku,
YOKOHAMA

SWITZERLAND

Stadthausgasse 18,
4051 BASEL

8 rue Verdaine,
1204 GENEVA

Augustinergasse 21,
8001 ZURICH

UNITED KINGDOM

191–197 Union Street,
ABERDEEN

10 Hale Leys,
AYLESBURY

187–195 High Street,
AYR

43 Market Place,
BANBURY

The Old Red House,
8–9 New Bond Street,
BATH

75 High Street,
BEDFORD

The Pavilions,
BIRMINGHAM

80 Old Christchurch Road,
BOURNEMOUTH

45 East Street,
BRIGHTON

62 Queen's Road,
Clifton,
BRISTOL

39 Broadmead,
BRISTOL

90–92 High Street,
BROMLEY

1 The Lexicon,
Cornhill,
BURY ST EDMUNDS

14 Trinity Street,
CAMBRIDGE

41–42 Burgate,
CANTERBURY

Queens West,
11 Queen Street,
CARDIFF

3–4 Grapes Lane,
The Lanes,
CARLISLE

10–13 Grays Brewery Yard,
CHELMSFORD

100 The Promenade,
CHELTENHAM

17–19 Watergate Row,
CHESTER

32 North Street,
CHICHESTER

4–5 Trinity Square,
COLCHESTER

11 Drummond Place,
CROYDON

8 Albert Street,
DERBY

5 The Broadway,
EALING

129–131 Terminus Road,
EASTBOURNE

90 George Street,
EDINBURGH

137 George Street,
EDINBURGH
(*Decorator Collection*)

126 Princes Street,
EDINBURGH

41–42 High Street,
EXETER

The Barn,
Lion & Lamb Yard,
FARNHAM

7 The Parade,
Metro Centre,
GATESHEAD

84–90 Buchanan Street,
GLASGOW

215 Sauchiehall Street,
GLASGOW

Old Cloth Hall,
North Street,
GUILDFORD

3 James Street,
HARROGATE

7 Commercial Street,
HEREFORD

121–123 Bancroft,
HITCHIN

3–4 Middle Street,
HORSHAM

17 Buttermarket,
IPSWICH

48–49 High Street,
KING'S LYNN

The Griffin,
Market Place,
KINGSTON-UPON-THAMES

108 The Parade,
LEAMINGTON SPA

Church Institute,
9 Lands Lane,
LEEDS

6 Eastgates,
LEICESTER

310 High Street,
LINCOLN

19–23 Cavern Walks,
Matthew Street,
LIVERPOOL

30 Great Oak Street,
LLANIDLOES

256–258 Regent Street,
Oxford Circus,
LONDON W1

71–73 Lower Sloane Street,
LONDON SW1
(*Decorator Collection*)

7–9 Harriet Street,
LONDON SW1

183 Sloane Street,
LONDON SW1

35–36 Bow Street,
Covent Garden,
LONDON WC2

157 Fulham Road,
LONDON SW3

36–37 High Street,
Hampstead,
LONDON NW3

Macmillan House,
Kensington High Street,
LONDON W8

8–10 King Street,
MAIDSTONE

28 King Street,
MANCHESTER

48 Linthorpe Road,
MIDDLESBROUGH

40–42 Midsummer Arcade,
MILTON KEYNES

45 High Street,
NEWCASTLE-UNDER-LYME

8 Nelson Street,
NEWCASTLE-UPON-TYNE

32–39 High Street,
NEWPORT,
Isle of Wight

108 The Parade,
LEAMINGTON SPA

Unit 3B Peacock Place,
NORTHAMPTON

19 London Street,
NORWICH

58 Bridlesmith Gate,
NOTTINGHAM

10 High Street,
OXFORD

26–27 Little Clarendon Street,
OXFORD
(*Decorator Collection*)

189–191 High Street,
PERTH

90 Queensgate Centre,
PETERBOROUGH

The Armada Centre,
PLYMOUTH

32 Fishergate,
PRESTON

75–76 Broad Street,
READING

68 George Street,
RICHMOND

13 Market Place,
ST ALBANS

49–51 New Canal,
SALISBURY

87 Pinstone Street,
SHEFFIELD

65 Wyle Cop,
SHREWSBURY

124 High Street,
SOLIHULL

2 Above Bar Church,
SOUTHAMPTON

107 High Street,
SOUTHEND

465–467 Lord Street,
SOUTHPORT

41–42 Henley Street,
STRATFORD-UPON-AVON

3–4 Times 2,
High Street,
SUTTON

164 The Parade,
Gracechurch Centre,
SUTTON COLDFIELD

19e Regent Street,
SWINDON

2–4 High Street,
TAUNTON

19–21 High Street,
TENTERDEN

61 Calverley Road,
TUNBRIDGE WELLS

1 The Parade,
High Street,
WATFORD

17 Grove Street,
WILMSLOW

126 High Street,
WINCHESTER

32 Peascod Street,
WINDSOR

54–55 Dudley Street,
WOLVERHAMPTON

Crown Passage,
Broad Street,
WORCESTER

28 Vicarage Walk,
Quedam Centre,
YEOVIL

7 Davygate,
YORK

SHOPS WITHIN
SAINSBURY'S
HOMEBASE

Winchester Road,
BASINGSTOKE

Pines Way,
BATH

762 Harrogate Road,
BRADFORD

Redlands Parkstone,
BRANKSOME

Colchester Avenue,
CARDIFF

St Andrews Avenue,
COLCHESTER

Junction Fletchamstead
Highway,
Sir Henry Parks Road,
COVENTRY

Stadium Way,
CRAYFORD

66 Purley Way,
CROYDON

Kingsway,
DERBY

St Oswalds Road,
GLOUCESTER

Priory Way,
Hessle,
HULL

714–720 High Road,
Seven Kings,
ILFORD

Felixstowe Road,
IPSWICH

King Lane,
Moortown,
LEEDS

37 Putney Road,
(off Welford Road),
LEICESTER

Syon Lane,
Isleworth,
BRENTFORD

10 Beckenham Hills Road,
Catford,
LONDON SE6

Rookery Way,
The Hyde,
Hendon,
LONDON NW9

473 High Road,
Willesden,
LONDON NW10

3 Station Road,
New Southgate,
LONDON N11

Fulborne Road,
Walthamstow,
LONDON E17

Oakfield Road,
Penge,
LONDON SE20

33 Brooks Lane,
NEWCASTLE-UNDER-LYME

229–253 Kingston Road,
NEW MALDEN

Victoria Promenade,
NORTHAMPTON

Castle Marina Park,
Castle Boulevard,
NOTTINGHAM

50 Halesowen Street,
Warley,
OLDBURY

23 Stadium Way,
(off Claydon's Lane),
RAYLEIGH WEIR

50 Kenavon Drive,
READING

Homested Retail Park,
Maidstone Road,
Chatham,
ROCHESTER

Rom Valley Way,
ROMFORD

Lordshill Shopping Centre,
SOUTHAMPTON

4 Great Portswood Street,
STOCKPORT

Quay Parade,
SWANSEA

Ing's Road,
WAKEFIELD

1 Bradford Place,
WALSALL

Sturlas Way,
WALTHAM CROSS

114 St Albans Road,
WATFORD

Hylton Road,
WORCESTER

North Wall District Centre,
Queensway,
WORLE

Junction Monkgate Foss Bank,
YORK

UNITED STATES

Crossgates Mall,
120 Washington Avenue, Ext.,
ALBANY, NY 12203

139 Main Street,
ANNAPOLIS, MD 21401

516 East Washington St.,
ANN ARBOR, MI 48104

29 Suburban Square,
ARDMORE, PA 19003

Lenox Square,
3393 Peachtree Road,
ATLANTA, GA 30326

Perimeter Mall,
4400 Ashford Dunwoody
Road,
ATLANTA, GA 30346

1224 Highland Mall,
6001 Airport Blvd.,
AUSTIN, TX 78752

Pratt Street Pavillion,
Harborplace,
BALTIMORE, MD 21202

203 Beachwood Place,
26300 Cedar Road,
BEACHWOOD, OH 44122

200–219 Riverchase,
Galleria Mall,
BIRMINGHAM, AL 35244

180 Town Center Mall,
BOCA RATON, FL 33431

83 Newbury Street,
BOSTON, MA 02116

1136 Pearl Street,
BOULDER, CO 80302

400 Commons Way,
Suite 117,
BRIDGEWATER, NJ 08807

23 Church Street,
BURLINGTON, VT 05401

Charles Square,
5 Bennett Street,
CAMBRIDGE, MA 02138

Carmel Plaza,
P.O. Box 2033,
CARMEL-BY-THE-SEA, CA
93921

Charleston Place,
146 Market St.,
CHARLESTON, SC 29401

South Park Shopping Center,
4400 Sharon Road, Sp. G-8,
CHARLOTTE, NC 28211

Barracks Road Shopping
Center,
CHARLOTTESVILLE,
VA 22901

148 Hamilton Place Mall,
2100 Hamilton Place Blvd,
CHATTANOOGA, TN 37421

The Mall at Chestnut Hill,
199 Boylston Street,
CHESTNUT HILL, MA 02167

8520 Germantown Avenue,
CHESTNUT HILL, PA 19118

Watertower Place,
835 N. Michigan Ave.,
CHICAGO, IL 60611

Kenwood Towne Center
R-19,
7875 Montgomery Road,
CINCINNATI, OH 45236

Galleria,
Towers-Erieview,
1301 E. 9 St.,
Suite G-308,
CLEVELAND, OH 44114

The Citadel,
750 Citadel Dr. E. 2008,
COLORADO SPRINGS,
CO 80909

1636 Redwood Highway,
CORTE MADERA, CA 94925

South Coast Plaza 2255,
3333 Bristol Street,
COSTA MESA, CA 92626

13350 Dallas Parkway,
Suite 1585,
DALLAS, TX 75240

423 North Park Center,
DALLAS, TX 75225

Danbury Fair Mall,
Suite 273,
7 Backus Avenue,
DANBURY, CT 06810

1439 Larimer Street,
DENVER, CO 80202

Kaleidoscope At The Hub,
555 Walnut St.,
Suite 218,
DES MOINES, IA 50309

Galleria Shopping Center,
3505 West 69th Street,
EDINA, MN 55435

11822 Fair Oaks Mall,
FAIRFAX, VA 22033

294 West Farms Mall,
FARMINGTON, CT 06032

Galleria Mall,
2492 East Sunrise Blvd.,
FORT LAUDERDALE, FL 33304

213 Hulen Mall,
FORT WORTH, TX 76132

58 Main Street,
FREEPORT, ME 04032

2153 Glendale Galleria,
GLENDALE, CA 91210

Woodland Mall,
3175 28th Street, S.E.,
GRAND RAPIDS, MI 49508

321 Greenwich Ave.,
GREENWICH, CT 06830

17100 Kercheval Place,
GROSSE POINTE, MI 48236

207 Riverside Sq. Mall,
Route 4 West,
HACKENSACK, NJ 07601

66 South Street,
HINGHAM, MA 02043

1450 Ala Moana Center,
Space 2246,
HONOLULU, HI 96814

Suite 2120,
5015 Westheimer,
HOUSTON, TX 77056

Suite 124,
1000 West Oaks Mall,
HOUSTON, TX 77082

8702 Keystone Crossing,
Fashion Mall,
INDIANAPOLIS, IN 46240

The Jacksonville Landing,
2 Independent Dr.,
Suite 155,
JACKSONVILLE, FL 32202

308 West 47th Street,
Country Club Plaza,
KANSAS CITY, MO 64112

The Esplanade (Mall),
1401 W. Esplanade,
KENNER, LA 70065

7852 Girard Avenue,
LA JOLLA, CA 92037

Victorian Square,
401 West Main Street,
LEXINGTON, KY 40507

Pavillion in the Park,
8201 Cantrell Road,
LITTLE ROCK, AR 72207

Century City Shopping
Center,
10250 Santa Monica Blvd.,
LOS ANGELES, CA 90067

Suite 739, Beverly Center,
121 N. La Cienega Blvd.,
LOS ANGELES, CA 90048

Louisville Galleria,
Space 109,
LOUISVILLE, KY 40202

2042 Northern Blvd.,
Americana Shopping
Center,
MANHASSET, NY 11030

Tysons Corner Center,
1961 Chain Bridge Road,
MCLEAN, VA 22102

Saddle Creek Shopping
Center,
7615 West Farmington Blvd.,
Germantown,
MEMPHIS, TN 38138

The Falls 373,
8888 Howard Drive,
MIAMI, FL 33176

The Grand Avenue,
275 W. Wisconsin Av. 5,
MILWAUKEE, WI 53203

208 City Center Mall,
40 South 7th Street,
MINNEAPOLIS, MN 55402

Ridgedale Center,
12711 Wayzata Blvd.,
MINNETONKA, MN 55343

Outlet Park at Waccamaw,
MYRTLE BEACH, SC 29577

The Mall at Green Hills,
2148 Abbot Martin Road,
NASHVILLE, TN 37215

260–262 College Street,
NEW HAVEN, CT 06510

333 Canal Street,
151 Canal Place Fashion,
NEW ORLEANS, LA 70130

Bowen's Wharf,
Avenue of the Americas,
NEWPORT, RI 02840

21 East 57th Street,
NEW YORK, NY 10022

714 Madison Avenue,
NEW YORK, NY 10021

398 Columbus Avenue,
NEW YORK, NY 10024

4 Fulton Street,
NEW YORK, NY 10038

979 Third Avenue,
2nd Floor,
NEW YORK, NY 10022
(*Decorator Collection*)

White Flint Mall,
11301 Rockville Pike,
NORTH BETHESDA,
MD 20895

2164 Northbrook Ct.,
NORTHBROOK, IL 60062

Twelve Oaks Mall,
27498 Novi Road,
Suite A,
NOVI, MI 48050

224 Oakbrook Center,
OAKBROOK, IL 60521

20 Old Orchard Shipping
Center,
SKOKIE, IL 60077

One Pacific Place,
OMAHA, NE 68114

Owings Mills Town
Center,
10300 Mill Run Cir. 1062,
OWINGS MILLS, MD 21117

320 Worth Avenue,
PALM BEACH, FL 33480

469 Desert Fashion Mall,
123 N. Palm Canyon Drive,
PALM SPRINGS, CA 92262

12 Stanford Shopping
Center,
PALO ALTO, CA 94304

221 Paramus Park,
PARAMUS, NJ 07652

401 South Lake Avenue,
PASADENA, CA 91101

1721 Walnut Street,
PHILADELPHIA, PA 19103

Biltmore Fashion Park,
2478 E. Camelback Road,
PHOENIX, AZ 85016

Shops at Station Square,
20 Commerce Court,
PITTSBURGH, PA 15219

Ross Park Mall, Space E3,
PITTSBURGH, PA 15237

2100 Collin Creek Mall,
811 No. Central Expwy,
PLANO, TX 75075

419 S.W. Morrison St.,
PORTLAND, OR 97204

Palmer Square,
46 Nassau Street,
PRINCETON, NJ 08542

2 Davol Square Mall,
PROVIDENCE, RI 02903

Crabtree Valley Mall,
4325 Glenwood Avenue,
RALEIGH, NC 27612

Galleria at So. Bay 172,
1815 Hawthorne Blvd.,
REDONDO BEACH, CA 90278

1404 Parham Road,
Regency Square Mall,
RICHMOND, VA 23229

The Commercial Block,
1217 East Cary Street,
RICHMOND, VA 23219

North Park Mall,
Suite 207,
1200 East County Line Road,
RIDGELAND, MS 39157

531 Pavillions Lane,
SACRAMENTO, CA 95825

267 Trolley Square,
602 East & 500 South,
SALT LAKE CITY, UT 84102

North Star Mall,
Suite 1224,
7400 San Pedro,
SAN ANTONIO, TX 78216

247 Horton Plaza,
Space 265,
SAN DIEGO, CA 92101

4505 La Jolla Village Drive,
Suite C 21,
SAN DIEGO, CA 92122

253 Post Street,
SAN FRANCISCO, CA 94102

1827 Union Street,
SAN FRANCISCO, CA 94123

Mainplace,
2800 North Main Street,
SANTA ANA, CA 92701

La Cumbre Galleria 109,
3891 State Street,
SANTA BARBARA, CA 93105

Valley Fair Mall,
Suite 1031,
2855 Stevens Creek Blvd.,
SANTA CLARA, CA 95050

696 White Plains Road,
SCARSDALE, NY 10583

F-331 Woodfield Mall,
SCHAUMBURG, IL 60173

405 University Street,
SEATTLE, DC 98101

The Mall at Short Hills,
SHORT HILLS, NJ 07078

87 Main Street,
SOUTHAMPTON, NY 11968

St. Louis Center C-380,
515 North 6th Street,
ST. LOUIS, MO 63101

74 Plaza Frontenac,
ST. LOUIS, MO 63131

Stamford Town Center 214,
100 Grey Rock Place,
STAMFORD, CT 06901

139 Main Street,
STONY BROOK, NY 11790

718 Village Circle South,
Olde Hyde Park Village,
TAMPA, FL 34606

2845 Somerset Mall,
TROY, MI 48084

1846 Utica Square,
TULSA, OK 74114

1171 Broadway Plaza,
WALNUT CREEK, CA 94596

3213 M. Street N.W.,
Georgetown,
WASHINGTON, DC 20007

Mazza Gallerie,
Chevy Chase,
WASHINGTON, DC 20615

85 Main Street,
WESTPORT, CT 06880

10861 Weyburn Ave.,
WESTWOOD, CA 90025

Merchants Square,
422 West Duke
of Gloucester St.,
WILLIAMSBURG, VA 23185

Twin Lakes Center,
WILMINGTON, DE 19807

740 Hanes Mall,
WINSTON-SALEM, NC 27103

290 Park Avenue North,
WINTER PARK, FL 32779

Woodbury Common Shopping
Center,

Jericho Tpke & Woodbury
Road,
WOODBURY, NY 11797

279 Promenade Mall,
6100 Topango Canyon Blvd.,
WOODLAND HILLS, CA 91367

108 Worthington Square,
Worthington Square Mall,
WORTHINGTON, OH 43085

Vanity Fair Mkt.,
Level 3,
Bldg 105, Hill Avenue,
Park road,
WYOMISSING, PA 19610

WEST GERMANY

Am Holzgraben 1–3,
5100 AACHEN

Karlstrasse 15,
8900 AUGSBURG

Tauentzienstrasse 21–24,
(Im Kadewe),
1000 BERLIN

Niedernstrasse 14,
4800 BIELEFELD

Sögestrasse 54,
2800 BREMEN

Hohestrasse 160–168,
5000 COLOGNE

Hunsrückenstrasse 43,
4000 DUSSELDORF

Goethestrasse 3,
6000 FRANKFURT

Neur Wall 39,
2000 HAMBURG

Georgstrasse 36,
3000 HANOVER

Kaiserstrasse 104,
7500 KARLSRUHE

Planken P3 12–13,
6800 MANNHEIM

Sendlingerstrasse 37,
8000 MUNICH

Ludgeriestrasse 79,
4400 MUNSTER

Ludwigsplatz 7,
8500 NURENBERG

Breite Strasse 2,
7000 STUTTGART

Langgasse 30,
6200 WIESBADEN

ACKNOWLEDGEMENTS

Illustrations are reproduced courtesy of the following photographers and institutions (figures in bold refer to page numbers):

1 Arabella Ashley © LA/W&N
2/3 David Garcia © LA
4/5 David Garcia © LA/W&N
6 David Garcia © LA/W&N
8 James Mortimer © LA
9 David Garcia © W&N
10 *left* David Garcia © LA/W&N; *right* National Gallery of Ireland
11 *left* Musée des Arts Decoratifs; *right* David Garcia © LA/W&N
13 *above* David Garcia © W&N; *below* Colin Jones © LA
14 Fritz von der Schulenburg
15 *Left* Victoria and Albert Museum, London; *right* John Miller © LA/W&N
16 David Garcia © LA
17 David Garcia © LA
18 *above* and *below* Arabella Ashley © LA
19 *left* Victoria and Albert Museum, London; *right* David Garcia © LA/W&N
20 Arabella Ashley © LA
21 *left* John Mason © LA; *right* Arabella Ashley © LA
22 Arabella Ashley © LA
23 Christine Hanscomb
24 Arabella Ashley © LA
25 David Garcia © LA/W&N
26 David Garcia © LA/W&N
27 Hazel Digby © LA
28 David Garcia © LA/W&N
29 Fritz von der Schulenburg
30 John Mason © LA
31 John Mason © LA
32 Victoria and Albert Museum, London
33 *left* John Miller © LA/W&N; *right* David Garcia © LA/W&N
34 *left* Bodleian Library, Oxford; *right* John Mason © LA
35 David Garcia © LA/W&N
36 *left* and *right* David Garcia © LA/W&N
39 Simon Brown © LA
40 John Miller © LA/W&N
41 O'Shea Gallery, London
42 *above* David Garcia © LA; *below* Syndication International/Country Homes and Interiors
43 David Garcia © LA/W&N
44 *left* Elizabeth Whiting & Associates; *right* David Garcia © LA/W&N
45 David Garcia © LA/W&N
46 *left* and *right* David Garcia © LA/W&N
47 *left* David Garcia © LA/W&N; *right* Charleston Trust
48 Fritz von der Schulenburg © W&N
49 *left* and *right* David Garcia © LA/W&N
50 Arabella Ashley © LA
51 Arabella Ashley © LA
52 Fritz von der Schulenburg © W&N
53 *above* David Garcia © LA/W&N; *below* Simon Brown © LA
54 Fritz von der Schulenburg © W&N

55 David Garcia © W&N
56 *left* British Library; *right* Arabella Ashley © LA
57 Fritz von der Schulenburg
58 David Garcia © LA
59 *left* David Garcia © LA; *right* David Garcia © LA/W&N
60 *above* and *below* David Garcia © LA/W&N
61 Fritz von der Schulenburg
62 *above* David Garcia © W&N; *below* David Garcia © LA
64 David Garcia © LA/W&N
65 *left* David Garcia © LA/W&N; *right* David Garcia © LA
66 David Garcia © LA/W&N
67 Fritz von der Schulenburg © W&N
68 Simon Brown © LA
69 *left* David Garcia © LA/W&N
   right John Miller © LA/W&N
70 *left* and *right* David Garcia © LA/W&N
71 David Garcia © LA
72 John Miller © LA/W&N
73 David Garcia © LA/W&N
74 David Garcia © LA/W&N
75 David Garcia © LA/W&N
76 David Garcia © LA/W&N
77 David Garcia © LA/W&N
78 Arabella Ashley © LA
79 *left* and *right* David Garcia © LA/W&N
80 *left* and *right* David Garcia © LA/W&N
81 David Garcia © LA/W&N
82 David Garcia © LA/W&N
83 *above* and *below* David Garcia © LA/W&N
84 *above* and *below* David Garcia © LA/W&N
85 Simon Brown © LA
86 *left* David Garcia © LA/W&N; *right* David Garcia © LA
88 *left* and *right* David Garcia © LA/W&N
89 *above* and *below* David Garcia © LA/W&N
90 David Garcia © LA/W&N
91 *above* and *below* David Garcia © LA/W&N
92 David Garcia © LA
93 Fritz von der Schulenburg © W&N
94 *left* Elizabeth Whiting & Associates; *right* Christie's Colour Library
95 Arcaid
96 Elizabeth Whiting & Associates
98 *left* Fritz von der Schulenburg © W&N; *right* Jeremy Whittaker © W&N
99 Fritz von der Schulenburg © W&N
100 *left* and *right* Fritz von der Schulenburg © W&N
101 David Garcia © LA/W&N
102 Fritz von der Schulenburg © W&N
103 *left* Elizabeth Whiting & Associates; *right* Michael Boys
104 Arabella Ashley © LA
105 Fritz von der Schulenburg © W&N

Artwork was produced by Lesley Sternberg/Sharp Practice.

INDEX